SCIENCE
Meets
FAITH

Edited by
FRASER WATTS

SPCK

First published in Great Britain 1998
SPCK
Holy Trinity Church
Marylebone Road
London NW1 4DU

The publisher acknowledges with thanks permission
to use the following:
Bloodaxe Books ('Glimpse', in *A Fragile City*,
Micheal O'Siadhail, 1995).
Bloodaxe Books ('Perspectives', in *The Chosen Garden*,
Micheal O'Siadhail, 1991).

British Library Cataloguing-in-Publication Data
A catalogue record for this book is available
from the British Library

ISBN 0-281-05112-7

Typeset by Pioneer Associates, Perthshire
Printed in Great Britain by
Arrowsmiths, Bristol

CONTENTS

To
Susan Howatch

PREFACE

Christian faith needs to be faithful to its inheritance, but it also needs to be rethought and stated afresh in the changing circumstances of each generation. The outlook of our own time has been affected more by the scientific developments of the last hundred years than by anything else. Christianity needs to take stock of these developments and to assess their implications.

Currently, there is great interest in this project, and a widespread hunger for guidance about how science affects Christian belief. There is also a growing band of scholars and thinkers devoting themselves to the dialogue between contemporary science and the Christian faith. I am personally enormously grateful to Susan Howatch, whose generous endowment of the 'Starbridge Lectureship in Theology and Natural Science' at the University of Cambridge has enabled me to devote myself to this task.

This book arises from two overlapping series of public lectures. First, in London in March 1996, there was a series of four lectures on Science and Religion, organized by the Reverend Dr John Bowker, the Gresham Professor of Divinity. The chapters in this book by John Bowker, Mary Hesse, Eugene d'Aquili and Andrew Newberg, and myself arise from that series of Gresham Lectures. I am grateful to John Bowker for his initiative in organizing them, and for his kind encouragement of this volume.

The lectures by John Bowker, Mary Hesse and myself were then repeated as part of a longer series in the autumn of 1996 at the Church of St Edward King and Martyr in Cambridge, where I am Vicar-Chaplain. This series also contained four fresh lectures which are also included here, by John Polkinghorne, Alan Cook, Derek Burke, and Daniel Hardy. To these, I have also added a general introductory chapter.

I believe the resulting book provides a good guide to the current dialogue between science and religion. Part One deals with issues arising from various particular areas of scientific enquiry, and each chapter is written by someone who has done distinguished work in the relevant science. Part Two stands back and seeks to put the current dialogue between science and Christianity in broader perspective.

Fraser Watts

ABOUT THE CONTRIBUTORS

Professor Eugene G. d'Aquili is Professor of Psychiatry at the University of Pennsylvania, Philadelphia.

The Reverend Dr John Bowker, formerly Professor of Religious Studies at Lancaster, is a Fellow of Trinity College, Cambridge, and Gresham Professor of Divinity in the University of London.

Professor Derek C. Burke was formerly Vice-Chancellor of the University of East Anglia.

Sir Alan Cook, FRS, was formerly Jacksonian Professor of Natural Philosophy in the University of Cambridge, and Master of Selwyn College.

Professor Daniel W. Hardy was formerly Van Mildert Professor of Theology in the University of Durham, and Director of the Center of Theological Inquiry at Princeton.

Professor Mary Hesse, FBA, was formerly Professor of Philosophy of Science at the University of Cambridge.

Dr Andrew B. Newberg is Fellow in the Division of Nuclear Medicine at the Hospital of the University of Pennsylvania.

The Reverend Dr John Polkinghorne, KBE, FRS, was formerly Professor of Mathematical Physics in the University of Cambridge, and President of Queens' College, Cambridge.

The Reverend Dr Fraser Watts is Starbridge Lecturer in Theology and Natural Science in the University of Cambridge, a Fellow of Queens' College, and Vicar-Chaplain of St Edward King and Martyr, Cambridge.

Chapter One

INTRODUCTION

Fraser Watts

When people meet each other, the conversation often begins with the question 'What do you do?' Since January 1994, when I took up the Starbridge Lectureship in the University of Cambridge, endowed by Susan Howatch, my answers to such questions have involved explaining that I teach the relationship between science and religion. I have discovered that this elicits surprise amongst most people who had no idea what I did and had not thought about these things before. People are intrigued that I should be trying to relate science and religion, but they think that I have got a tough job on my hands, because they assume that science and religion are in conflict, if not incompatible.

For the last hundred years or so, this has been the received wisdom about the relationship between science and religion. If you examine the idea more carefully it breaks down into three subcomponents that we can call substantive, philosophical and historical.

It is assumed that there is conflict between science and religion on a number of *substantive* points, such as how the world came into being. Science claims one thing, that the world came into being through the Big Bang, and species came into being through evolution by natural selection. Religion is thought to make quite different substantive claims, that God created the world in seven days. Thus there seems to be a conflict over substantive claims. It seems that one or other has got to be wrong.

Next it is assumed that there is *philosophical* conflict, or conflict about the basis of truth. It is assumed that science arrives at its claims by investigation and experiment, and thus that scientific knowledge is based on what we can establish as being true.

Religion, in contrast, is thought to be based on revelation from God, and to be mediated by human faith. These are such different bases for claims about what is true that it seems once again that science and religion are bound to be on a collision course.

Third, it is widely assumed that there is a *historical* conflict between science and religion, and has always been. The story is thought to be one in which the forces of religion, reactionary forces, have tried to keep science at bay, but that they have failed to do so, and now science has won. According to this story, the historical relationship between science and religion is strewn with examples of conflict between the two, those involving Galileo and Darwin being the most celebrated.

Now, I will argue that the real relationship between science and religion is more complicated at each of these three points. I will claim that there is no necessary conflict over substantive matters, once you understand the different questions that science and religion are answering; they are giving different answers to different questions, rather than different and conflicting answers to the same questions. Second, I will claim that both science and religion are rational in their somewhat different ways, and that there can be mutual respect between them. Third, I will point out that the idea that science and religion have always been in conflict is an invention of the late nineteenth century, and that the truth about their historical relationship is much more complex.

Substantive Conflict

Religion must take most of the blame for the idea that there is conflict between science and religion over their substantive claims. The trouble is that the claims of religion have all too often been presented in a simplistic way that invites misunderstanding. Even when church leaders (such as David Jenkins, former Bishop of Durham) have tried to correct this, they have been misrepresented by the media as giving up altogether on key religious claims, rather than trying to clarify the nature of those claims.

Much of the supposed substantive conflict focuses on origins. How did the world come into existence? How did species come into existence? The first two chapters of the book of Genesis seem to give answers to these questions that are in conflict with scientific ones. However, this is to misunderstand what Genesis is about, and the kind of material that is to be found in its early chapters. Genesis was never meant to be a scientific textbook, and its early chapters are not trying to answer modern scientific questions.

The early chapters of Genesis have been widely held to contain 'myths' — though that is also a misleading word. The person in the street assumes that a 'myth' is simply wrong. However, when biblical scholars say that the creation stories in Genesis are 'myths' they are making a more subtle point. They are saying that they convey truths, but that relatively abstract truths are being conveyed in concrete, story form. The truth of the creation myths lies in what they point to about the dependence of the world on God, not in the details of the story.

It gets us into roughly the right ball-park to think of them as parables. The Gospels, as everyone knows, contain many parables. The details of Jesus' stories about the kingdom of heaven are not meant to be true as historical fact; they are meant to point to truths about God and humanity. Parables have been described as 'earthly stories with heavenly meanings'. The same could be said about the creation myths at the beginning of Genesis.

The general point that the Genesis creation myths are making is that the world owes its existence to God, and came into existence as a result of his loving, creative purposes. The details of the stories are relatively incidental, and largely serve just to make that general point. One of many reasons for thinking that the authors did not take the details of the story too seriously is that Genesis includes, in chapters 1 and 2, two separate creation stories which make similar general points but which are different in detail. If they were taken as scientific accounts of the origin of the world, they would be in conflict with each other.

These are not new points. Already, in the fifth century, St Augustine, in his commentary on Genesis, recognized that there might be points at which Genesis, if taken literally, would come into conflict with what was known in other ways to be true. He had no compunction in urging that in such circumstances Genesis should be taken metaphorically, though still as conveying truths of a different, more analogical kind. It is interesting that one of the reasons he urges for this is that taking every detail of the Scriptures literally risks bringing their core message into disrepute. Galileo was drawing on Augustine when he quipped that the Bible 'teaches us how to go to heaven, not how the heaven goes'. Augustine's warning is relevant today to those Christians who feel honour bound to uphold the literal truth of every detail in the Bible.

Some have tried to reconcile the Genesis story of the origin of the world with modern science by taking the six 'days' it describes in a very general way as referring to epochs. Taken in this way, the sequence in the Genesis story corresponds in a rough-and-ready way to what would be accepted scientifically. However, this way of reconciling things runs the risk of obscuring the nature and purpose of the Genesis myths. Their interest and importance do not depend on whether or not they get the scientific story roughly right, but on the general point they are making about the relationship of creation to God.

Science and religion are answering different questions about the nature and origin of the world. It has sometimes been said that science is answering 'How?' questions, while religion is answering 'Why?' questions. That is helpful as an initial way of making the distinction between them, though it should not be taken in too absolute a way. Science does not only answer 'How?' questions and religion does not only answer 'Why' questions. However, it is helpful in making the point that science and religion are generally answering different questions, rather than giving conflicting answers to the same questions.

Philosophical Conflict

When it comes to the more philosophical conflict about the different approaches to truth of science and religion, there is blame on both sides. There has been a tendency to misrepresent the approaches to truth of both science and religion in a way that exaggerates the difference between them.

Let me first put into perspective some of the exaggerated claims that are sometimes made for science as a path to truth. In doing so, I do not want to be misunderstood as denigrating science in any way. It has been enormously important as a way of expanding our horizons and increasing our knowledge. Moreover, I have devoted a large part of my working life to scientific research. However, that does not stop me thinking that some of the exaggerated claims made for science need to be recast in a more subtle way.

On the grandiose view, science is an absolutely dependable

way of tackling questions. Whatever has been shown to be true scientifically is beyond all doubt and can be trusted as being absolutely true for all time. Also, on this grandiose view, there is no way of reaching truth other than science. Further, we are well on the way to getting answers to all real questions through science. On this view, anything that cannot be answered scientifically is not a proper question, even if it may look like one.

This bold view of science, associated with the philosophical movement known as logical positivism, and dominant in the middle of the twentieth century, is on the way out. It has been steadily undermined at various points. We have come to realize that scientific observation is not quite as objective as it seems. What observations science makes and how they are interpreted depends on the theoretical perspective of the scientists concerned. Moreover, scientific theories are never conclusively proved to be true; they are just the best ways of making sense of the data for now. Science can be seen to go through periodic radical changes of theoretical perspective, in which what was once thought to be firmly established gets recast in a new light. The replacement of Newtonian dynamics by quantum dynamics is the most dramatic example of the century. Finally, the sciences are themselves quite diverse; not all sciences are based on experiments for example. There is thus no single scientific method, and no sharp dividing line between the natural sciences and other forms of enquiry.

I want to argue that religion has its own form of rationality. Clearly religion is not science, and it does not pretend to be. It does not have the same rationality as science. But neither is it wholly irrational. It finds its place within the broad family of rationalities.

In arguing this, I need to clear away some misunderstandings about the nature of religious faith. There are some, like Kierkegaard, who see faith as being 'blind'. Far from regarding that as a problem, they think that the irrationality of faith is the most splendid thing about it. On this view, if there were any *reasons* for faith, it would not be faith at all, but something inferior. Needless to say, it suits those such as Dawkins who wish to attack religion to assume that faith is blind. I see faith differently. There *can* be rational support for religious faith — though it can never be wholly based on reason. Religious faith is not just believing that there is a God; it is a practical, living trust in God. However, it is not *un*reasonable; it is perfectly sensible to ask whether it squares with what we know about the world.

Up to a point the rational grounds for religious faith are similar to the rational grounds for holding scientific theories. The background assumption of most religion, that there is a God, is rather like the background assumption of a broad scientific research programme.

Broad background assumptions often play an important part in underpinning scientific research programmes. For example, much seventeenth-century science assumed that matter was essentially composed of little particles. Whatever scientific question arose, the assumption was that it had to be solved in terms of the action of little particles. Why does acid have a sharp taste? Because there are little particles like tiny needles pricking the tongue. Why does a powder dissolve in liquid? Because the particles of the liquid attack the particles of the powder. And so on.

The background assumption that the material world was composed of particles was not tested as such, it was simply assumed. However, it was not an irrational view, it fitted a good deal of data and proved fruitful for quite a while. Even though it was not directly based on evidence, it was not impervious to it, and was eventually modified under the pressure to accept a broader class of explanations.

Belief in God, the background assumption of all theistic religion, is rather like the seventeenth-century assumption that the world is composed of particles. Belief in God cannot be proved, but it makes sense of a broad range of data, and is at least a rational view of the world. In this, it is like the broad background assumption of scientific research programmes.

The distinctive thing about religious rationality is that it provides a way of integrating and making sense of a very broad range of considerations. It brings together, for example, the beauty and fruitfulness of the natural world, personal religious experience, and the kind of claims to revelation associated with Jesus of Nazareth. It is rationally defensible to suggest that all these are explicable in terms of the same God. Like the view that the world is composed of small particles, it goes beyond the data, but connects with it and makes sense of it.

History of Conflict

The idea that science and religion are necessarily in conflict is often bolstered with the claim that, historically, they always have been in conflict. The story is told of how science was opposed by the Church at its dawn at the beginning of the seventeenth century. Galileo's persecution by the Roman Catholic authorities is often cited as the prime evidence of this. The story continues, with the Church trying to hold back scientific advance at every point, culminating in the fierce opposition it put up to Darwin's theory of evolution in the latter part of the nineteenth century.

This story is now generally discredited amongst serious historians of the relationship between science and religion. It stands in need of radical correction at too many points to be defensible.

Perhaps the first point to make is that there is no evidence that the relationship between science and religion has always been seen in terms of conflict. The conflict idea arose in the late nineteenth century in the aftermath of controversies over Darwin's theory of evolution. As often happens, the sense of conflict at that time was projected backwards, and history was re-written to defend the idea that the relationship had always been one of conflict. T. H. Huxley, for example, remarked that 'extinguished theologies lie around the cradle of each new science'.

Both science and religion changed radically in the nineteenth century from what they had been before. The very word 'science' only took on its current sense of natural or experimental science in the nineteenth century. Though it is often claimed that the scientific revolution occurred in the seventeenth century, the methods of enquiry that developed then were not generally referred to as science at the time. They would more likely have been seen as natural or mechanical philosophy. To call them 'science' is another piece of re-writing of history. Moreover, science as anything like a modern profession only came into existence in the nineteenth century. Before that time, much scientific investigation was carried out in other contexts, the majority of investigations into natural history being undertaken by clergymen.

Also, radical rejection of religion in Europe only became at all widespread in the nineteenth century. Of course, there had been various kinds of religious dissent before, arising first between Catholicism and the newer Reformed traditions, later between the rather general Enlightenment religion known as 'deism' and more traditional forms of Christianity. Though the term 'atheism' was coined in the Enlightenment, it was only in the nineteenth century that religion was at all widely rejected in favour of atheism or agnosticism.

Before the nineteenth century, most Western scientists, like everyone else, were Christians of some kind or other. Moreover, many of the great early 'scientists' took religion very seriously. It is now recognized that the seventeenth century was not characterized by a growing divorce between science and religion, but by an unprecedented integration of the two. There are many examples of this that could be given, but a few will have to suffice.

Kepler was both a Copernican and also someone who developed elaborate ideas about the significance of his cosmology for his Trinitarian theology. Galileo, though he rejected some of the conservative thinking of the Catholic church, had strong views about biblical interpretation and how it related to cosmology. He wrote at length about it, in a way that was much indebted to Augustine, in his letter to the Grand Duchess Christina. Newton was also deeply religious, dividing his time between scientific and theological research and regarding both as equally important. At many points, his theological views helped to shape his scientific theories. For example, he saw 'absolute' time and space as a manifestation of the eternal God. Such examples make a nonsense of the idea that science and religion have always been in conflict.

The controversy over Darwinism was rather different in that a scientific theory was used for the first time to spearhead a movement against conventional religion. This was not really Darwin's own doing, more that of Huxley, whose agnosticism was combined with a fierce antipathy to religion, especially to the leading curchmen of his day. However, even here there has been re-writing of history. The celebrated debate between Huxley and Bishop Wilberforce at Oxford in 1860 did not make the impact at the time that is widely assumed. The accounts we have of it come only from Huxley's side, and were only set down long after the event.

Though there was undoubtedly religious opposition to Darwin, the situation was more complicated than is often assumed. There were also many leading churchmen who in different ways saw no difficulty in reconciling Darwinism with Christian belief, the main line of argument being that natural selection was God's way of creating species. Also, not all reservations about evolution by natural selection came from the religious quarters. There were also serious scientific doubts too, especially about whether human beings had evolved from other species.

Mutual Support?

The idea of unmitigated conflict between science and religion does not stand up to examination at any level. Of course, there are elements of conflict, but the story of the relationship between science and religion is too complex to be summarized simply in terms of conflict. Whether you look at conflict over substantive claims, philosophical conflict over rationality, or the history of the relationship between science and religion, the story cannot be told solely as one of conflict. How else then should the relationship be characterized?

Some people have wanted to turn the story right round and to argue that the relationship between science and religion is one of mutual support, that the Christian religion has given rise to science, and that science in turn supports the Christian religion. This is also, in my view, a simplistic characterization of the relationship — though there are certainly lines of argument that can be adduced in its favour. It is worth mentioning some of them.

Some go back to bedrock characteristics of Christian thinking, and to very early aspects of the Christian tradition. One key factor is that Christianity has never had the negative attitude to the material world that some other religions have had, especially the religious traditions of India. Because of the central doctrines that God created the material world and that God in Christ took a material form, it has never been possible for Christianity to take the view that the material world is not worth studying. Another bedrock Christian assumption that was clearly set out in the early centuries is that the world is lawful and orderly. It is therefore worth trying to discover the nature of this lawfulness. Further, the lawfulness of the world is held to be contingent in the sense that God could well have created it otherwise. Because of this contingency, it is appropriate to discover the nature of the world's orderliness empirically.

As one might expect from these assumptions, the early Fathers of the Church were generally well disposed to empirical investigation in fields such as cosmology. They sometimes sensed that the speculative cosmologies of their time were in conflict with their Christian assumptions, but assumed that there would be no conflict with anything that was shown empirically to be the case. Because of this, they tended to favour an empirical approach to cosmology over a speculative one.

It is arguable that these basic assumptions in the Christian tradition help to explain why science eventually developed most powerfully in the Christian West — though it does not explain why it was not until the seventeenth century of the Christian era that anything like modern science developed. But when modern science did eventually develop, there were certainly mutually supportive assumptions. It was assumed that God had revealed himself in two ways, in two 'books', the book of the Scriptures and the book of nature. God's revelation could be studied in both, and the scientific study of the natural world was seen almost as a kind of act of worship.

Moreover, it was thought that science could provide rational support for Christian beliefs about God. Central to this was the argument from design, an argument deployed in a previous era by Aquinas and others, but now applied with new force. It was assumed that science, in providing evidence for the orderly and well-adapted nature of the universe was gradually accumulating evidence that it had been designed. Moreover, the qualities of design discerned in the universe were thought to provide evidence for the Christian God who had designed it. In this way, it can be argued, science which had come from basic Christian assumptions, was returning to give rational support to Christian beliefs.

This kind of argument, known as 'natural theology', took slightly different forms in the biological and physical sciences. In the biological sciences, there was particularly strong emphasis on how remarkably well adapted many living forms were for the environments in which they flourished. This suggested that they had been designed for these environments, for example camels had been designed for the desert. In turn the mechanistic science of the seventeenth century was thought to be uncovering the laws of nature that reflected the mind of the God who had created it. However, it was assumed that mechanical laws could never explain how the living universe was upheld in being. The living God was invoked to breathe life into the universe and to uphold it in being.

Of course, this close, symbiotic relationship between science and religion did not last. For one thing, science developed in ways that were not foreseen by the natural theologians of the seventeenth century, and key assumptions of their arguments became untenable. Increasing evidence of enormous changes in the earth's crust and in living species was difficult to square with the initial assumption that God had created the universe perfect, and therefore that it was in need of no further change. The development of theories of evolution by natural selection provided an alternative explanation of why living forms were so well adapted to their environment. Also, it increasingly seemed that mechanical science might be able to provide an adequate explanation of the physical world by itself, without invoking God as an extra principle.

There now seems no going back to the comfortable synthesis of science and theology of the Enlightenment. This is not only because of the way science has developed. In fact, some of the remarkable facts about the 'fine-tuned' universe discussed by John Polkinghorne in Chapter Two are at least consistent with the presumed purposes of a creator God. More fundamentally, it was probably always a mistake to try to start from scientific facts and to reach religious conclusions. To do so distorts the nature of faith and the nature of God.

Faith is fundamentally a matter of personal commitment, though it is also a rationally defensible view of the world, and the arguments of natural theology neglected this. Also, our knowledge of God is assumed to come about through his revelation of himself to us. The natural theology of the Enlightenment tried to apply to the study of God the observational methods that were being so successful in natural science. In fact, religion is very different from science. Knowledge of God is not based on observation in the same way as the conclusions of natural science, though it can be expected to be consistent with observational knowledge.

It was another weakness of Enlightenment natural theology that, at best, it provided arguments for an intelligent creator God, that is, for some general kind of theism. There was always an enormous gulf between the beliefs of the Christian religion and what could be supported by natural theology. Not only did it distort the nature of both faith and God, but it never delivered anything like the broad range of conclusions that would be needed if scientific support for Christian theology were to be successfully delivered. In fact, religious believers would be unwise to imagine that science could deliver such support, though they should be concerned with whether science gives a picture of the world that is consistent with their religious faith.

Independence or Dialogue?

Those who conclude that religion and science are neither in conflict with one other, nor offering each other strong support often conclude that they are completely unrelated. Indeed, this is probably the most common position among scientists who are also religious. Independence is usually achieved by dividing up the territory. Some things fall into the sphere of religion, where they can be undisturbed by science. Other things fall into the sphere of science where they can be undisturbed by religion.

Historically, this reflects a view of religion that has become increasingly common since the scientific revolution in the seventeenth century. Increasingly, life has become compartmentalized, with a variety of specialized domains, and religion has become one of these. Before that, distinctions were made more in terms of perspectives or frameworks than in terms of compartments. The religious, or theological, perspective was brought to bear on the whole of life, but it was not the only perspective.

One way of trying to maintain harmony between science and religion is to keep them in their separate territories. If science and religion each have their own territory, and keep to it, they can be kept out of conflict. Though this seems attractive in some ways, it is a *modus vivendi* with which neither can really be satisfied. The religious perspective on life is peculiarly comprehensive. Because there is nothing that is outside the life of God, there can be nothing that is outside a religious frame of reference. If religion becomes merely a specialist domain of ecclesiastical or moral activity, it is retreating to something much narrower than the life of God.

Equally, science has broad ambitions. Though we should not endorse the old grandiose view of science that it is the only reliable way of answering any question, we should defend the capacity of science to make its distinctive contribution to the investigation of anything whatsoever. Religion and morality, for example, can both be investigated scientifically, though the scientific perspective is not the only one.

There is another reason why science and religion cannot be confined to their separate compartments and ignore each other. They are each concerned with truth, and there cannot be multiple truths which are completely unconnected with each other. There is one world, and any valid truths are truths about the same one world. Admittedly, they may be concerned with different aspects of the world, or be approaching questions from different perspectives, but the issue is bound to arise of whether an approach to truth from one perspective squares with an approach from another. If, as I believe, science and religion both involve approaches to truth, albeit of very different kinds, they cannot just ignore each other. They have to consider whether and how their perspectives on truth are consonant with one another. They need to stay in contact, and to engage in conversation.

That is why there is a need for books such as this one, which bring science and religion into relation with one another. The dialogue between them can take two different forms, and there is a need for both.

One is concerned with substantive issues, and Part One of this book is devoted to some of the key issues that arise on the interface between religion and science. The five chapters in the section are organized around particular areas of scientific enquiry, moving from the physical sciences, through evolutionary biology, to the human sciences.

It is worth noting here that religion has a very different relationship with different sciences. Though the physical sciences once seemed to be the most inconsistent with a religious perspective, that has changed dramatically over the last hundred years. There is now a remarkable openness to religious concerns in the physical sciences, and a movement towards consonance that would once have seemed incredible. That is reflected in the chapters by Polkinghorne and Cook. In contrast, the biological sciences are currently much more antagonistic to religion. This is partly because of their tendency to make comprehensive and exclusive claims about the nature of human beings.

A hallmark of this is the tell-tale phrase 'nothing but'. Some evolutionary biologists see human beings as nothing but survival machines for their genes, while some neuroscientists see them as nothing but bundles of neurones. However, as the chapters by Burke and Watts argue, there is no reason at all why the human and life sciences should make such strong and exclusive claims. Indeed, far from being a necessary feature of the human sciences, it can be argued that such over-bold claims are themselves unscientific. These issues come particularly to the fore in the scientific study of religion, reflected here in the chapter by d'Aquili and Newberg on the neurological substrate of religion. Such a theory does not show that religion is 'nothing but' a particular mode of operation of the physical brain.

The second part of the book returns to more general issues about the nature of science and of religion, and the consequences of this for their relationship. These general issues have been opened up in this introductory chapter, but the three chapters that constitute Part Two return to them at a more advanced level. Bowker and Hesse, in different ways, both look at the historical, philosophical and sociological relationship between science and religion. In the final chapter, Hardy looks at the nature of religious thinking and at our understanding of God. The dialogue between science and religion has all too often been beset by simplistic theology, and a healthy conversation between them needs to be more attentive to the nature of religious thought.

PART ONE

Starting
From
Science

Chapter Two

BEYOND THE BIG BANG

John Polkinghorne

The topic is 'beyond' and not 'before'. When Augustine was faced with the question of what was God doing before the act of creation, he rejected a frivolous response (preparing hell for the curious) and emphasized instead that there was no 'before' since time came into being along with the rest of creation. The universe was not created 'in time' but 'with time'. Fifteen centuries later, Einstein agreed. General relativity links together space, time and matter, so that modern cosmology understands them to have a common origin.

To look beyond the Big Bang is to ask, with Leibniz, the profound question, 'Why is there something rather than nothing?' It is also to decline to agree with Hume that it is sufficient to treat the physical world as a brute fact requiring no further explanation. Instead, we shall see that science's account of the laws of nature, far from appearing intellectually self-contained, actually raises metaquestions, going beyond science's unaided power to answer but meaningful and necessary to ask, which force themselves upon our attention. I shall suggest that to look beyond the Big Bang is to enter a realm where the doctrine of creation, in its Judaeo–Christian–Islamic articulation, has significant things to say.

To see that this is so one must first dispose of a most unfortunate misapprehension that seems to afflict many cosmologists when they seek to garnish their writings with some simple 'theological' reflections. The error is to believe that the doctrine of creation is concerned with the physical question of temporal origin ('Who lit the blue touch paper of the Big Bang?'), whilst in fact its focus is on ontological origin (Leibniz' question about why anything exists at all). Stephen Hawking seems to believe that if his interesting speculation that the universe has a finite

17

age but no datable moment of origination were to prove correct, then somehow the Creator would have been put out of a job. Of course, this is just an elementary theological mistake. God is as much the Creator today as fifteen billion years ago, performing the divine work of holding the universe in being. To adopt Hawking's words at the end of *A Brief History of Time*,[1] the issue is whether God has been continually 'breathing fire' into the beautiful but abstract equations of fundamental physics in order to maintain a world whose physical fabric they actually describe. The question of whether a doctrine of creation is a credible belief today will not turn on conjectured details of very early cosmic history but rather on whether the whole of that history can be understood as indicating the presence of a divine Mind and Purpose behind it.

Cosmologists and particle physicists believe that the truly fundamental nature of the physical world is expressed in a highly symmetric ur-structure, a Grand Unified Theory (GUT) of great elegance and economy whose actual form is presently unknown to us. This act of faith is appealing, and I certainly share the hope that the belief expressed is true. It involves trust in the power of the human mind to penetrate reality beyond that which we immediately encounter. Only in the highly energetic moments of the very early universe would there be a regime of such high energy as to allow the GUT to manifest itself unmasked.

Almost immediately after the Big Bang, expansion would have cooled the world down to temperatures at which the forces of nature as we experience them today would have begun to crystallize out. As part of that process there is thought to have been a brief but highly significant period of cosmic expansion, occuring at a rate greatly exceeding that of the more stately regime that has followed it. This conjectured and hectic 'boiling' of space is called the inflationary era. Believing that it occured is another act of cosmological faith, but one that is well-motivated. Certain consequences would have followed from this process which do seem to correspond to features of the universe observed today. One of these concerns a property of our world without which we could not have evolved during its long fruitful history: the very close balance that exists between the expansive force of the Big Bang throwing matter apart and the cohesive force of gravity pulling matter together. If expansion had predominated by only a tiny fraction, then the universe would rapidly have become too dilute for any process leading to the formation of complex structure to have been possible; if gravity had predominated by only a tiny fraction, then the universe would have re-collapsed before there had been time for any process of complexification to bear fruit. Our human existence depends upon there having been this inflationary process in the very early universe (well before it was 10^{-30} seconds old), which itself depends upon the presumed GUT having had a form which enabled this to happen.

The need for the laws of nature to be capable of producing an inflationary-induced balance between expansion and contraction is but one example of how special the physical fabric of the universe has to be if its evolutionary history is to lead to the coming-to-be of life. It is not 'any old world' that can produce systems of the complexity of us human beings. This insight, that the potentiality for the evolution of carbon-based life had to be present in the particular fundamental physical structure of the universe from the Big Bang onwards, is called the anthropic principle. Every period of cosmic history illustrates this fruitful 'fine-tuning' of the laws of nature in our world. In the first three minutes, when the whole universe was hot enough to be the arena of nuclear reactions, the balance between the nuclear forces had to be just right to ensure that, at the end of this brief but hectic era, there should be some hydrogen and not just helium left in the gross structure of cosmic matter. Not only would no hydrogen have meant eventually no water (with its many remarkable properties, essential to life) but also there would have been no hydrogen-burning stars. The latter have two vital roles to play in making the evolution of life possible. One is to act as long-lived reliable energy sources. Biological evolution on Earth has been fuelled for four billion years by the steady burning of our local star, the Sun. This process of stellar energy supply is controlled by a delicate balance between two of the forces of nature, gravity and electromagnetism. If that balance had been slightly different, stars would either have been too cool to be effective or they would have burnt so fiercely that they would have become exhausted after a mere few million years, a period quite insufficient to allow life to develop.

The second indispensable role of the stars is to be the providers of the chemical raw materials of life. The very early universe is simple and only has simple nuclear consequences, supplying the two simplest elements, hydrogen and helium. They do not have a rich enough chemistry to be on their own the building blocks of highly complex systems. For that, one needs the heavier elements, most of all carbon with its ability to form the long chain molecules which are the basis of biochemistry. There is only one place in the whole universe where such elements can be formed: in the interior nuclear furnaces of the stars and in the trauma of a supernova explosion at the end of certain stars' lives. Every atom of carbon in our bodies was once inside a star; we are all made of the ashes of dead stars. One of the great triumphs of twentieth-century astrophysics has been to unravel the process of stellar nucleogenesis. It turns out to depend in a beautiful and highly sensitive way on the details of the nuclear forces. The slightest change in the nature of those forces would have disrupted the chain and made the evolution of biological life an impossibility, frustrated by a lack of the necessary chemical material.

One could continue with many more examples making up the tale of the intrinsic fine-tuning which has enabled evolutionary fruitfulness. It is time, however, to ask the question, What do we make of it? Is it just our luck that the laws of nature were propitious? Here we encounter the first example of a metaquestion, arising from scientific insight but pointing beyond it to a deeper level of enquiry. Science just assumes the laws of nature as the unexplained ground of its understanding of the details of physical process. Yet we have seen that those laws have so remarkable a character, so closely related to the universe being able to become aware of itself through the evolution of conscious life, that it does not seem adequate to treat them as 'brute fact' in the way that David Hume recommended. If the potentiality for our existence had in some real sense to be present at the time of the Big Bang itself, is it enough to regard our being here as just a 'happy accident'? Of course there are many contingent aspects of human existence – it is not being suggested that from all eternity it was decreed that *Homo sapiens* should have five fingers – but the evolution of some form of conscious carbon-based life does not look at all like an accident.

One of the philosophers who has thought about these matters with helpful carefulness is John Leslie. Not only does he get the science right, but also he makes his philosophizing accessible by framing it in the form of stories. Leslie is a parabolic philosopher. In his book *Universes*, he tells the following tale: You are about to be executed. You are tied to the stake, your eyes are bandaged, and the rifles of ten highly trained marksmen are pointed at your chest. The officer gives the order to fire and the shots ring out . . . You find you have survived! What do you do? Shrug your shoulders and say, 'Well, that was a close one'? Certainly not, for so remarkable an experience surely calls for interpretation. Leslie suggests that there are just two possible rational explanation of your good fortune. One is as follows. Maybe many, many executions are taking place today. Even the best of marksmen occasionally miss and you just happen to be in the one where they all miss. If there are enough executions taking place today (and there would have to be a very large number), this is a conceivable rational explanation. There is, however, a second possibility. Maybe more was happening than you had realized. The marksmen were on your side. They missed by design.

It is easy to see how this little tale translates into the consideration of anthropic fine-tuning. First, there is something to be explained in so remarkable a circumstance. It is intellectually lazy, not to say foolish, just to exclaim, 'We're here because we're here' and leave it at that. Two possible explanations can be entertained. One is that maybe there are many, many different universes, each with its own set of natural laws. If there are enough of these independent worlds (and there would certainly have to be a lot) then in one of them, by chance, circumstances could be just right for the evolution of carbon-based life. That is the one in which you and I live, of course, because we could appear in the history of no other. This is the many worlds interpretation of anthropic fine-tuning. But there is an alternative interpretation. Maybe there is only one universe which is the way it is, in its finely-tuned anthropic fruitfulness, because it is not any old world but rather a creation endowed by its Creator with precisely the physical fabric that will enable it to fulfil the divine purpose of a fruitful evolutionary history. This interpretation offers a revival of the argument from design, but in a totally different and revised form. No longer are we dealing with William Paley's divine craftsman, forming creatures as a watchmaker forms a watch, but with a Creator who builds fruitful potentiality into the basic structure of a universe which is then allowed 'to make itself' (the theological way of understanding evolution). This insight meets Hume's criticism, that the argument from design is too anthropomorphic in its character, for there is no human analogue to God's gift of anthropic potency.

It also expresses a right relationship between theology and science, with the former complementing the latter by offering an intellectually satisfying answer to the metaquestion raised by the anthropic principle.

Both of these proffered explanations are metaphysical in character. Science has no direct knowledge of other worlds beyond that of the universe of its observation, and God is beyond its immediate ken also. Leslie believes that each interpretation carries equal persuasive power. Either there are many worlds and/or there is a God. I think that this fifty-fifty judgement is correct if we are simply talking about the anthropic principle on its own. Yet I believe that there are also other reasons for believing in God and then the anthropic argument can become part of a cumulative case for theism. One of those other reasons relates to another metaquestion arising from science.

The simplest way of stating it would be to ask, 'Why is science possible at all?' Of course, we must be able to understand the world around us to a certain extent in order to enable our successful survival in the struggle for life. Yet, it by no means follows that we have to possess the astonishing intellectual powers that allow us to comprehend the vast space–time structure of the cosmos or the idiosyncratic and unpicturable strangenesses of the quantum world. The mystery deepens when we recognize that it is mathematics which provides the key to unlock the secrets of the physical world. The great theoretical physicist, Paul Dirac, was not a conventionally religious man. He was once asked what was his fundamental belief. He strode to a blackboard and wrote that the laws of nature should be expressed in beautiful equations. Mathematical beauty is not something that everyone has very ready access to but I can assure you that among those of us who speak the language it is something that we can recognize and agree about. It has always been found to be present in fundamental physical theories. Dirac made his wonderful discoveries through a lifelong search for beautiful equations.

When we use mathematics in this way, as a tool for scientific discovery, something very surprising and significant is happening. It scarcely seems enough to say that it is just a piece of luck for those with mathematical skills that things work out this way. Cosmologists and other scientists have discovered that the physical world that originated in the Big Bang is rationally beautiful and rationally transparent to us. We live in a universe shot through with signs of mind. A coherent and attractive explanation of that fact is that it is indeed, as people like Stephen Hawking like to say, because the Mind of God lies behind the rational order of the cosmos. Science is possible because the universe is a creation and we are creatures made in the image of our Creator.

I do not present the deep intelligibility of the world as a knockdown argument for God's existence. We are in a realm of discourse where such arguments are not available to either theist or atheist. I do present it, however, as a coherent and satisfying insight. I would never think of my atheist friends as being stupid, but I do believe that theism explains more than atheism does.

Candour requires that I go on to acknowledge another insight of the cosmologists which at first sight seems to call into question the claims so far being made to discern a divine Mind and Purpose behind cosmic history. It is possible to peer not only into the past of the universe, but also into its anticipated future. On the very largest scale, the process of the cosmos is a gigantic tug-of-war between the two opposing tendencies of expansion and gravitational attraction. We have already seen how evenly balanced they are and we do not know which will win in the end. In consequence, two alternative future scenarios need to be considered. In one, expansion prevails. In that case, the present expansion of the galaxies will continue for ever. Within each galaxy, matter will condense into gigantic black holes, which over unimaginably vast periods of time will decay into low-grade radiation. That way the world ends with a whimper. If, on the contrary, gravity prevails, what began with the Big Bang will end with the Big Crunch as the universe collapses back on itself again. That way, the world ends with a bang. Either way, the universe is condemned to ultimate futility. Carbon-based life will prove but a transient episode in cosmic history. Considerations of this kind prompted the distinguished theoretical physicist, Steven Weinberg, to proclaim that the more he understood the universe, the more it seemed to him to be pointless.

What is the religious believer to make of that? It is a serious issue and I personally am not disposed to seek a solution along the lines proposed by the cosmologist, Frank Tipler. In his book, *The Physics of Immortality*,[2] Tipler suggests a highly speculative scheme by which 'life' could engineer increasingly more bizarre ways of processing information. In the closing super-energetic dying moments of a collapsing cosmos, Tipler believes that carbon-based life would have given way to an ever-faster racing 'cosmic computer', capable of processing an infinite number of bits of information. Because he takes the reductionist view that we are ourselves no more than computers made of meat, Tipler envisages that this fantastic prospect would provide a satisfactory fulfilment to the history of the universe. I think otherwise. For me the tale of the eventual futility of physical process is a reminder that if there is a true hope that in the end all will be well (and it is, I believe a deep human intuition that this is the case), its ground must lie outside the world as science knows it. Only the faithfulness of the everlasting God can be the basis for a hope that goes beyond, not only our individual human death and decay, but also the death and decay of the universe itself. Only the steadfast will of the Creator can ensure that the Big Bang was not an empty explosion fated to return again into eventual nothingness.

I have suggested that we can and should take with all due seriousness all that cosmology can tell us about the past history and future prospects of the wonderful and fruitful universe in which we live. Rather than conflicting with religion, these scientific insights raise metaquestions, going beyond science's competency to answer, but meaningful and demanding a response from those who, like all scientists, are embued with a thirst for understanding. I have proposed that religion can provide coherent and intellectually satisfying answers to these questions. The root of the matter lies in deciding whether the universe's history is ultimately just a tale told by an idiot (as Weinberg seems to believe) or whether we truly live in a cosmos which, despite present perplexities, will be found in the end to make total sense. It is my religious faith that enables me to take the more hopeful view. I believe that the really Grand Unified Theory, the true Theory of Everything, is not some set of beautiful equations which we might hope one day to write on our T-shirts, but theology itself, with its account of the God who is the Sustainer of the physical world and the Ground of creation's eventual fulfilment. That is the meaning of the process that was set in motion at the fiery explosion of the Big Bang, fifteen billion years ago.

Chapter Three

UNCERTAINTIES OF SCIENCE

Alan Cook

Introduction

My aim in this chapter is to give some idea of the meta-physical basis of the scientific study of the natural world (ourselves included), and to indicate how far the results of science may be secure and how far uncertain. Uncertainties in science come about on the one hand because of limitations on the observations we can make, and on the other hand, because the natural world itself may behave in unpredictable ways.

Revelation offers accounts of the origin and nature of ourselves and the world in which we live. So does the scientific study of the natural world, but by different means and with autonomous aims. The results of the respective approaches have led to much dispute, frequently intense, ever since modern science as we know it began to be independent of revelation, and especially since Galileo and his colleagues and successors. If we are properly to appreciate the argument we need to understand what are the valid claims of science. Peacocke has observed, with reference to Christian doctrines of creation, 'any doctrine of creation, if it is not to become vacuous and sterile, must be about the relation of God to, the creation by God of, the world which the natural sciences describe'.[1]

Much the same may be said of the practical application of Christian teaching of ethics and morals in the actual world in which we live. Whether we are trying to understand creation or whether we are concerned to live out the Christian life, we must do so in and about the world that the natural sciences describe.

The gospel for the Sunday next before Advent is the parable of the master going on a journey who left with his servants five talents, two, and one; and required of them an account when he returned. Our Lord spake it as he himself was about to go on a journey, to his crucifixion. He left his disciples with their talents. He leaves us with our talents, until he comes again. Others in this series of lectures have implied, or have said explicitly, that we have to employ our talents in this world as it is. We shall not make the most of them unless we have a true understanding of this world and of our brothers and sisters in it, an objective knowledge of things as they are, not muddled by thoughts of how we might like them to be. The Christian use of science is to display the reality of the world, however it has come to be, in which we are put to exercise our talents.

Radical changes in the scientific view of the world and in the understanding of its claims, have come about because of developments in the years around 1900; they have implications for the consistency or inconsistency of revelation and natural science, and for living the Christian life in the world as it is.

Science aims to give our knowledge of the natural world a rational structure and to confirm it by predicting observations as yet unmade, and testing them against the event. Robert Boyle, the guide of natural philosophers in the revolutionary years at the end of the seventeenth century (the revolution in science, that is) described a successful scientific theory: 'It enables a skilful Natural Philosopher to foretell future phenomena by their Congruity or Incongruity to it and especially the Events of such Experiments as are aptly devised to Examine it; as Things that ought or ought not to be Consequential to it.'[2]

Behind that apparently straightforward statement lie some arguable presuppositions. Most people, most practical scientists, assume that there is a natural world that exists independently of whether or not you or I are observing it – or at least we behave in that way. Working scientists, consciously or not, are almost all philosophical realists, like most Christian theologians, who accept that God exists, whether or not they are there to think about him.

Scientists are not, however, naïve realists. Most now recognize that they never have a direct knowledge of that independent world, the knowledge they have is of their *observations* of it, by no means the same thing. The human condition and the natural world, each constrains and distorts the observations that we can make. Thus when we try to place our observations into the framework of a rational theory, and test it in the way that Boyle set out, the theory we construct and test is a theory of our observations, not strictly speaking of that independent world of which they are a refracted representation.

Is then a successful prediction from a theory a demonstration that the theory does represent in some sense the independent world and not just the existing observations of it? It seems plausible that it is, but it is difficult to construct a rigorous argument.

John Locke was one of the first to distinguish clearly between our ideas and the sensations on which they are founded, and between the external world and our sensations of it. Newton was alert to those distinctions. When he commented on some observations by Halley of colours of things seen under water, he wrote of 'red-making rays' distinguishing the sensation of red from the properties of the light that produced it.[3] We today are often far less discriminating.

Newton developed his dynamical theories in order to account for the motions of bodies in the solar system under their mutual gravitational attractions, and to show that no other force was necessary. For many years dynamics was effectively restricted to the study of the behaviour of mechanical systems, but nowadays we recognize that it has far wider applications; it is the mathematical study of how things change and is not restricted to mechanics or physics. The power of Newton's mathematical model of dynamics came increasingly to dominate people's thoughts; they lost sight of Locke's distinction, and came to believe that the independent world itself evolved according to Newton's principles. At the same time Linnaeus, Ray and others showed that there was order in the variety of forms of plants and animals; and the Scriptures, subject to textual, historical and literary criticism, were seen to be writings with human failings, not infallible revelation.

Enlightenment philosophers, contributors to the French *Encyclopédie*, especially its editors, Diderot and d'Alambert, became convinced that the natural world was autonomous and rational and could be fully understood and securely predicted if only observations were sufficient, and logic, especially mathematics, powerful enough. That confidence in the power and autonomy of science, bolstered by successful prediction in the form of novel works of engineering, prevailed until the end of the nineteenth century – and still does in blind reliance on the technological fix. It was famously expressed by the French mathematician Laplace, who after explaining his system of celestial mechanics to Napoleon, was asked by the Emperor, 'But where does God come in?'

'Sire, I have no need of that hypothesis.'

Relativity

Three more or less simultaneous developments at the end of the nineteenth century undermined that assurance: relativity, quantum mechanics and chaotic dynamics. All raise questions of what we can know beyond our observations, and of what we can predict of observations as yet unmade, whether through limitations of knowledge, or because the natural world itself behaves unpredictably.

Classical physics itself has limitations, as in so-called inverse problems, of which there are important examples in the study of the Earth. We can measure various quantities over the surface, the value of gravity, the magnetic field and so on. What can we learn from them about the internal structure of the Earth which produces them? We can make definite calculations of the surface properties generated by a given internal structure, we cannot derive a unique internal structure from the surface properties, only a range of allowable structures.

Relativity[4] is a formal theory corresponding to the fact that the only way whereby we can know about distant events is by sending out to them electromagnetic signals, radio signals or light rays, and receiving electromagnetic signals back from them. Although we can assign separate independent times and positions to events in our immediate neighbourhood, we cannot do so for distant events, for which we only know times of emission and reception of signals to and from them. Those signal times may be consistent with a range of times and positions that we can assign to the distant events. We can choose the values we give to the times and positions of the events subject only to the condition that they lead to the observed times at which electromagnetic signals are emitted and received. The allowable times and positions of the events are related by a mathematical prescription known as the Lorentz transformation. That is the simple basis of special relativity. It is not quite all. Electromagnetic signals can carry more information than just times, and the Lorentz transformation applies to other pairs of quantities than times and positions, for example, the frequencies and wavelengths of light waves, or electric and magnetic fields.

In special relativity we take the speed of the light that brings information from a distance to be a constant, not because we know that it is, but because we cannot test, out there, that it is not. In some rare cases it is plain that the speed of light does vary, for instance when a light ray passes very close to the Sun, and then special relativity has to be extended so that the speed of light can depend on masses along the path – that is, general relativity.

Special relativity also applies to electromagnetic forces between microscopic particles. Changes in the forces are transmitted with the speed of light, and when particles change their relative positions, the electromagnetic forces between them take time to adjust to the new configuration; in addition, when the forces change they alter the velocities of the particles. The consequences of special relativity in microscopic physics are the phenomena associated with spins of elementary particles.

Lorentz transformations belong to a class of mathematical operations known as representatives of groups. Groups and their representatives are very important in physics because they ensure that, as with the Lorentz transformation, certain quantities, usually related to our observations, remain unchanged in theoretical calculations. They can also express the fact that the natural world often shows symmetry, as in the structure of crystals. The microscopic world is also highly symmetrical, in part a consequence of special relativity, and that shows up for example in the discrete frequencies of the light that atoms emit.

The message of relativity is that because the world is such that we can only learn about distant or microscopic events through electromagnetic signals, questions about when or where did a particular event occur have no unique answer; in that form they are invalid questions.

Inverse problems and relativity, in different ways, exhibit limitations on our knowledge of the world that are imposed by our place in the world and by the means for exploring the world that nature itself affords us. If there were no electromagnetic radiation, we should not have the actual theory of relativity.

Quantum Mechanics

Observers and experimenters have long recognized that their results are always uncertain, that observations never repeat exactly, because things are not absolutely cold, instruments are imperfect, scientists are human and careless, and for many other reasons. Observations therefore never agree exactly with predictions of theories, but that does not mean that comparisons of theory and observation are futile. The theory of probability enables us to estimate the likelihood of being wrong when we say that some observations do or do not confirm a hypothesis. When the design of an experiment is thorough and sophisticated and observations are careful, the result can have a high and assignable probability. We always hope to improve our results by careful attention to the deficiencies. One of the elements of quantum mechanics is that the act of observation is inherently uncertain, beyond any possible technical refinement. The very act of observation alters the state of the thing observed, and further, the result of two successive observations may depend on the order in which they are made. In classical physics, the order of observations is supposed to be irrelevant, but quantum mechanics takes explicit account of the difference in its mathematical form and expresses it in terms of a little quantity called Planck's constant that puts a natural limit on the reliability of any physical measurement, although it is a limit never so far attained in practice.

Quantum mechanics, like relativity, is a model of our observations of the independent world. Both are written in terms of quantities such as times and positions in relativity, or wavefunctions in quantum mechanics, that on the face of it could be given values in that independent world. It is not so. Those quantities are strictly elements of the theory; they enable us to calculate the results of observation, such as the observed times in relativity or the wavelength of light from a sodium lamp; they cannot ever be observed; and they can be changed according to rules such as the Lorentz transformation that leave unaltered the observations related to them.

Relativity and quantum mechanics have made us appreciate the limitations placed on our knowledge of the world by where we are in the world, by the means we have to observe it, and by the way in which our observations may change it. The behaviour of the independent world is not necessarily uncertain, our observations of it are, and the limitations upon those observations determine in important ways the forms of theories, and so help to explain why mathematical theories are so successful.

Many of our observations of the physical world are dominated by symmetry. Crystals have symmetry, so do molecules, in that our observations of them are independent of the direction from which we observe them. Given that there exist protons and nuclei and electrons, the possible stable atoms are determined by conditions of symmetry, and so are possible molecules. Our observations of the physical world thus appear as a mathematical system. There is much to be said for a Pythagorean view of the physical world, or rather, our observations of it, as a realization of mathematical structures. Relativity and quantum mechanics have not reduced the predictive power of physics, rather they have turned it in somewhat different directions, respecting the limitations to which they are subject. Within those limits the predictions of relativity and quantum mechanics are sometimes verified to an extraordinarily close degree. Relativity and quantum mechanics have not made classical physics obsolete, quite the contrary, they have shown why it is so successful over its proper field of things that are not too far away, nor moving too fast, nor too small.

Chaotic Dynamics

Towards the end of the nineteenth century the Parisian mathematician, Henri Poincaré, the brother of the First World War politician Raymond, was investigating the stability of the solar system. It was not a new problem, it had occupied outstanding mathematicians over centuries and was still unsettled. Might the planets all eventually fall into the Sun, or might they, on the other hand, fly off into space? The equations that make up the mathematical model of the solar system are differential equations, statements of the rates at which things change, in the solar system the velocities of the planets in their orbits about the Sun under their mutual gravitational attractions. The equations seemed to give the correct behaviour of the planets over short periods of time – thousands of centuries – but what happened after very long times was unclear.

Solutions to differential equations depend on the form of the equation but also on the state from which you start, the initial conditions. The equations take you from that initial state to some later one, and in well-behaved equations, such as the majority that appear in physics, there is a clear relation between the first state and the last. A change at the beginning leads to a well-defined change later on; changes in the final state are commensurate with those in the initial state.

Poincaré found that the equations for the solar system did not behave in that regular way. Changes in the initial state could apparently give rise to quite incommensurate changes in the final state, such that the two states seemed to bear no relation one to the other. Sometimes a very small change in the initial state could produce a large and unpredictable change in the final state, but in other systems, the final state would always be much the same whatever the starting point. Those sorts of behaviour are now called chaotic.

Chaos is not really a good term, for it suggests complete disorder, as in primeval chaos. The equations, however, are not disordered nor vague; it is certain aspects of their consequences that are irregular. The equations belong to an orderly world of equations, but the solutions to a disorderly world of response. No better name than chaos has found favour, and it is here to stay. It is useful to speak of deterministic chaos, for that reminds us that the equations which lead to it are definite and unambiguous, although the solutions to them are not.

Chaos follows from complexity, complexity in the structure of a system, and complexity in the forms of the equations that relate the elements of the system to each other. There are nine planets in the solar system, all attracted by the Sun and each attracted by all the others, a far more complex structure of relationships than if there were just one or two planets. Beyond that the simple gravitational attraction between any two planets is modified by the common attraction of the Sun, with correspondingly complex equations for their respective accelerations. Similar conditions apply far beyond the solar system, widely in biology and in human systems in economics and politics.

The mathematical notion of linearity is crucial. It means that if more than one cause is acting, the effect of them together is obtained by simply adding together the effects of each separately. Many equations of physics are linear, and a fundamental assumption in quantum mechanics entails a linear equation for the rate of change of a wavefunction.[5] Non-linear behaviour is different; the effects of multiple causes do not just add up but combine in more complex ways, as products or powers for instance.

Complex structures and non-linear interactions are the main causes of deterministic chaos, but not the only ones. If the ranges of variables are bounded, the behaviour of a system after encountering a boundary may not be predictable.

Poincaré himself pointed out that weather systems were unpredictable, for the dynamics of fluids is essentially non-linear and interactions in the atmosphere are complex. There may be some success in predicting the weather over a few days, but prediction beyond about three weeks is physically impossible. A further important example of deterministic chaos in physics is the behaviour of the main magnetic field of the Earth, which reverses its polarity at irregular intervals from tens of thousand to millions of years. The main field is almost certainly generated by the interactions of fluid motions, electric currents and magnetic fields in the liquid core of the Earth, highly non-linear processes, and the switch from one more or less stable state to the other is characteristic of deterministic chaos.

Chaotic systems can behave in various distinct ways, of which four are particularly important. The one most familiar from popular accounts is when an imperceptible change of initial conditions produces a very large effect, the result of the remote butterfly flapping its wings. A switch from one definite state to another, as with the geomagnetic field, may occur as the result of some small change of circumstances. There may be quasi-stable states where nothing changes and that are approached (but maybe never attained) from wherever the system may start. They are called attractors. Yet again, some chaotic systems oscillate, not with a single definite period, but with one that is statistically constant.

Most physics is not obviously chaotic. In principle physics probably is chaotic, but only very weakly, and rarely significantly, which is why physical theories are very effective at prediction and why chaotic behaviour was not appreciated before Poincaré; no one up to then had noticed it in physics. No more than relativity and quantum mechanics has deterministic chaos supplanted classical linear physics; like them it has shown why it works so well within its proper field.

Biology seems to be inherently more complex than physics, both in the structure of relationships and in their form. Biological processes often involve many linked pathways with non-linear interactions, just the conditions for deterministic chaos. The first biological system to be studied mathematically was the annual catch of fish in the northern Adriatic. Vito Volterra in the 1920s showed that the catches could be represented by the solutions of a non-linear equation, the Lottke–Volterra equation. Later, the catches of Arctic hares in the Hudson Bay area were matched by solutions of another non-linear equation, the logistic equation. Those are examples of the dynamics of the relations between predators and their prey – lynxes hunt the hares, but the lynx population declines when they deplete the hares overmuch, which then recover. More generally they are examples of interactions between populations, or population dynamics, among them epidemics such as measles, malaria and AIDS. They might be called external population dynamics, concerned with populations of whole organisms; there are in addition internal population dynamics concerned with molecules and cells within an organism. The response of the immune system of a mammal to infection can be represented by chaotic models, as can the onset of an auto-immune disease, in which the immune system attacks something necessary for the health of the organism itself. Thus the organ that produces insulin is attacked in certain forms of diabetes, and the linings of joints in rheumatoid arthritis.

Chaotic behaviour may be at the root of biological evolution. Evolution comprises various distinct topics. There is the evolution of complex processes of physiology and metabolism; there is the evolution of organs, such as eyes and ears; there is the co-evolution of complementary structures in plants and animals, such as the slender structure of a particular flower adapted to the long beak of a particular humming bird. Many people have suggested that chaotic processes underlie evolution, and some mathematical models have been produced for certain evolutionary processes, but a great deal more waits to be done on fundamental problems, especially as ideas of chaos are sometimes injected in rather vague general ways when strict mathematical models should be developed.[6]

Few would dispute that once a variant has occurred Darwinian processes will determine whether or not it persists. But how does it come about in the first place, by pure chance, like the monkey at the typewriter evolving Shakespeare's plays, or perhaps in some cases more like an unforeseen chaotic switch from one stable state to another? Many people associate evolution especially with the development of new species. Again, once a new species has come into being, fitness in Darwin's sense will determine whether or not it survives, but how a new species first appears is not so clear. A species is a population of individuals that can reproduce itself in a stable way for very many generations. More precisely, with sexual reproduction, a species is a pair of populations that may be thought to interact in a deterministic chaotic manner. It seems to me that the formal study of evolution requires a mathematical model of how such a stable pair can occasionally produce another pair of populations with fertile offspring but unable to interbreed with its progenitors. Once again, a chaotic switch seems possible, and it may be that it could be triggered by some external condition.

It is possibly misleading to speak of external conditions as if they were something independent of the evolving organisms. Animals, for example, evolve under the external conditions of the plants around them, but the plants equally evolve under the conditions maintained by animals. No less are the physical conditions independent of biological evolution, for animals and plants affect the hydrodynamics of shallow seas, and plants and animals effect geological changes. Mathematical models may be helpful in understanding limited aspects of evolution, but it should not be supposed that the mathematical model has remained the same throughout the course of evolution when in fact it may have changed as a result of changes in the so-called external conditions.

In most chaotic behaviour there is no well-defined relation of a final state to an initial state. The two are disconnected. If the final state of a dynamical system is uniquely related to the initial state, the latter may be inferred from the former and the dynamics is reversible, the operation that takes A to B has an inverse that takes B to A. If B is not uniquely related to A then no such inverse can be defined. That excludes a very large class of mathematics that depends on there being an inverse and which is very powerful in the physical sciences.

I have insisted that scientific theories are strictly concerned with observations and not with the independent world itself. That is true for chaotic dynamics; at the same time it seems plain that the independent world, and not just models of it, has chaotic properties, for it has the characteristics that entail chaotic behaviour, complex structures, non-linear relations, and bounds.

Chaotic dynamics has manifestations beyond the natural sciences. If individuals and groups interact in complex ways, as they do, then economic and political activity may be expected to show chaotic features. It is not difficult to think of examples of the four main types; some economic phenomena have been studied as instances of quasi-periodic behaviour.

Implications

It might seem that if the behaviour of the world is in some sense unpredictable, then the usual way of confirming or falsifying scientific theories by comparing prediction with outcome is not possible. If a mathematical model correctly represents in its structure some natural chaotic system, and both are chaotic, the behaviour of each will be unpredictable, and consequently agreement between them cannot be expected. Yet while each may be unpredictable in detail, there are properties that may be comparable. The statistical properties of the behaviour of a system controlled by deterministic chaos are different from those of one following purely random chance. There may be quasi-stable states, or quasi-periodic oscillations. As is explained in more detail in the Appendix in the section on constraints and freedom in deterministic chaos, the structure of a mathematical model determines the classes of behaviour that it may follow, the existence of fixed points, and other general features. In that sense deterministic chaos is deterministic. Within that deterministic framework the course followed in any particular case may be undetermined.

The classical epistemology of science, such as the falsifiability concept of Karl Popper, has to be re-stated in terms that take account of the predictable aspects of deterministic chaos as well as of its unpredictable aspects, but is not to be discarded, particularly as much of physics is not significantly chaotic.

Chaotic ideas do not get us off any epistemological hooks. Laplace's epigram, 'I have no need of that hypothesis', is as valid now as when he uttered it, more so indeed, for notions of chaos go far to show how Laplace's orderly world can encompass the disorderly, how the result of well-determined interactions can be unpredictable. Why should someone get a particular form of diabetes, and someone else stay healthy? We may never be able to trace the details of the cause in each case, but have, nonetheless, a good general idea of how one can be afflicted and another not. To rephrase Laplace, 'We are having less and less need of that hypothesis.'

The most significant theological consequences of the appreciation of chaos may lie in ethics and pastoral theology. Chaos tells us that in many fields of human activity it may be, indeed it is so, that either we cannot tell what may be the outcome of our actions, political or economic, or of grandiose technological adventures; or alternatively, whatever we do, it will make no difference. Much traditional ethical theory and pastoral theology depends upon the assumption, explicit or implicit, that we can predict the consequences of an action, make a realistic assessment of its good and bad effects, and hence choose the action with the best (or least bad) outcome. Whether we are guided by atheistical utilitarians or by priestly spiritual directors, chaos in human affairs seems to destroy the basis of such nice calculations. Are we not indeed closer to the position of the Greeks of the classical world, as set out by Bernard Williams in his recent book *Shame and Necessity*?[7] The Greek gods, powerful and capricious, might stand for the personifications of a chaotic world in which we are playthings. How should we behave in a world that we can neither predict nor influence, and in which our actions may have effects quite different from those we intend? Should not moral theologians be re-examining the Christian Scriptures and Fathers to reformulate principles of moral behaviour in an unpredictable world?

What can be said of the origins of a chaotic world? If the present state of a system, of the universe itself as a whole, is not uniquely related to an earlier state, what definitively can be said about the earlier state from a study of the present one? It seems to me possible that the question of the origin of the universe, attractive as it is to extrapolate back in time by known physics, is a question to which there is no answer, at least not from within physics. Just as the fundamental axioms of mathematics cannot be established by arguments from within mathematical logic, it may be that the origin of our physical universe cannot, in principle, be established by physical arguments.

If God created an orderly world with chaotic properties, what was his purpose? can he be said to be omniscient? and can we envisage him acting in the world to guide its evolution? They are not new questions, they are like the question of free will, but extended to the material world. If the structures of atoms and molecules are determined by symmetry, the big discontinuity is the emergence of life and the jump from the structure of large molecules to the role of DNA. The subsequent evolution of living creatures may very well have depended on chaotic processes, with the available paths at any point established by the state already reached. If so, then the most that God could have done would have been to set up conditions that might lead to sentient life and creatures that could discuss how they came into being, but would not have ensured that they did. We can say that God created the world, but we cannot say how he brought it into its present state. I do not think that our present understanding of chaotic processes is adequate for any purely scientific assessment of ideas of the intervention of God in the natural world such as have recently been discussed by Professor Polkinghorne and Dr Peacocke.[8] We may have less and less need of 'that hypothesis' but we are still very far from understanding deterministic chaos well enough to say if it may leave opportunities for divine intervention in 'the world which the natural sciences describe'. Here as in moral theology, notions of chaos do not, so I think, raise any new profound questions, rather they reinforce and deepen existing ones.

Conclusion

I have made three points. First, the knowledge of the independent world that science can give us is constrained by the nature of the world itself and by the human situation. Those constraints are at the same time part of the reason for the power of mathematical physics, and because physical theory is often very effective in prediction it probably corresponds to actual aspects of the independent world.

Physics, which is only marginally chaotic, and biology which seems inherently chaotic, together show that the world has deterministic structures but that its behaviour is not pre-determined in detail.

Some aspects of chaotic behaviour are unpredictable, others are not wholly so. Together they raise ethical questions of personal and public behaviour.

The evolution of the world, physical and biological, may have followed a course in which the possible paths at any point were not determined in a purely random way, but were set by the structure of the world at that point. The switch between paths may have been a chaotic event. God could have established the conditions that led to the evolution of sentient creatures, but could not have ensured that it happened.

Discussions of the implications of the scientific representation of the natural world for philosophy and theology run the risk that terms with precise technical connotations in science may be used metaphorically in other fields of discourse within which their meaning is not precisely defined – discussions of the implications of relativity have suffered in that way in the past. Ferrière and Fox, writing of the application of chaotic notions to the study of evolution, observed that 'that the jargon of non-linear dynamics can obfuscate, rather than clarify, when divorced from its mathematical roots' and warned against treating mathematical ideas as vague metaphors.[9] The warning is even more necessary in discussions of the relation of natural science and theology.

I return to my beginning, to leave you with a wider vision than the astringent aphorism, 'We have less and less need of that hypothesis.' However the world may have come into being, and whether or not we have less and less need of that hypothesis, it is here in this present world that we have to live out Christian lives. To do so we need to know the natural world and our fellows in it as they are, warts and all.

I gave the lecture on which this chapter is based on Thanksgiving Day, the day when our cousins in the United States remember the first harvest the pilgrims reaped, the fruits of the talents given to them in that particular land to which they had come.

This is the place, here and no other, to which we have been brought to do God's will. Those are the salt plains, the snow-capped mountains, those the bleak moors and the hidden gardens; there is the desert for us to bring to flower, that the lion to be led to lie down with the lamb.

This is the Place: here we are set down to serve the Lord; we must spy out the land.

APPENDIX

I did not have time in my lecture to refer to, far less discuss, two topics which are relevant to my general argument but which are still not clearly understood. They are the relation of quantum mechanics to deterministic chaos, and the constraints upon the evolution of a chaotic process.

Quantum mechanics and deterministic chaos

Quantum mechanics is fundamentally a linear theory. A basic axiom asserts that states of a system combine in a linear way; in consequence the equation for the evolution of the wavefunction in time is a linear equation. Similarly the mathematical operations on the wavefunction which represent the results of observations of a quantum system are linear operations. There are arguments about whether or not a quantum system can behave in a chaotic manner, but I do not think they affect any of my discussion in

the lecture. That is not because biological systems and processes, as well as physical systems and processes, are not in the last
analysis, quantum systems and processes. The whole natural
world obeys quantum mechanics. Deterministic chaos enters
through the correspondence between quantum dynamics and
classical dynamics.

There is a mathematical transformation that relates the
eigenvalues of quantum operators to classical variables. Furthermore the evolution of the wavefunction in time is determined
by the Hamiltonian operator which for the most part corresponds formally to the classical Hamiltonian function. Chaotic
dynamics deals with the deterministic relations between classical
variables; the unpredictable outcomes arise in the classical
domain, not in the underlying quantum domain. There may be
exceptions to that general statement. Classical electrodynamics
is replaced by quantum electrodynamics for subatomic particles,
and has to be supplemented by quantum chromodynamics; if
there is chaotic behaviour peculiar to quantum mechanics, its
source may lie in those more complex interactions.

Constraints and freedom in deterministic chaos

The state of a system at any time can usually be specified by the
values of an appropriate number of variables, of which the
evolution in time is governed by equations for the rates of
change of those variables. At any one time the state of the system may be represented by a point in a multi-dimensional space
(phase space) having co-ordinates corresponding to the values
of the variables. The behaviour of the system may be pictured
as a trajectory of the point moving in time. The general problem of deterministic chaos can be said to be the classification of
the types of possible trajectory.

There will in general be multi-dimensional surfaces (lines in
two-dimensional space) on each of which the rate of change of
one variable will be zero. Those surfaces divide the whole of
phase space into cells in which the rates of change of the variables maintain their signs. Where the surfaces intersect, more
variables than one have vanishing rates of change. In two
dimensions there may be one or more points of intersection,
fixed points, at which the rates of change of both variables are
zero. Similarly in three or more dimensions there may be one
or more points at which all surfaces intersect and all rates of

change are zero. Poincaré classified fixed points in two and three dimensions, but little is known of their characteristics in more dimensions.

The ranges of the variables that describe a system are usually restricted by external restraints (the food supply or physical space might limit a population of hares or blood cells) so that the cells in the space of variables are defined by external boundaries as well as by the internal surfaces on which rates of change are zero.

A chaotic system that conforms to the foregoing description is deterministic in the sense that the partition of phase space into cells is determined by the equations for the rates of change and by the external boundary limits, as likewise are the location and nature of fixed points. The system will be chaotic if of all the possible trajectories, the one that is followed depends upon imperceptible changes in initial conditions.

It seems likely that any system that must be described by a large number of variables (more than six or seven, perhaps) will show chaotic behaviour. That is because the number of neighbours of any one cell increases with the square of the number of variables, and therefore so does the number of ways by which a trajectory may pass from a cell to a neighbour. Consequently quite small changes in the way in which a trajectory enters a cell may lead to a qualitative difference in the subsequent course of the trajectory. Furthermore a similar indeterminacy occurs whenever a trajectory crosses a cell boundary. It is not just that the trajectory is unrelated to the initial state of the system, but that at every subsequent state the course followed is indeterminate.

An important question is whether a fixed point of a system will ever actually be attained. The existence of fixed points and the general behaviour of trajectories in relation to them has been fully analysed for two variables, but far less is known about systems of three and more variables.

In summary, a deterministic chaotic system is deterministic in the sense that the possible classes of trajectory and fixed points follow from the forms of the governing equations and the external constraints, and it is chaotic in the sense that any particular trajectory does not so follow.

Chapter Four

EVOLUTION AND CREATION

Derek C. Burke

My contribution concerns two major themes in Western thought; two themes that have generated enough books to fill a small library! Yet I have a few thousand words! So some of what I say will therefore of necessity seem superficial to some – for I am not a trained philosopher; and some of it will seem obscure – for many readers will not be trained scientists. However, I will do my best.

Let me first say what I mean by creation. I shall restrict myself to the creation of all living beings, and I shall not be discussing the creation of the universe, that was John Polkinghorne's task. I shall take the account in the first chapter of Genesis as the basis of Christian thinking on this subject. I shall not be discussing its critical status, although I personally regard it as an authoritative religious account. That is to say, I do not regard it as a scientific account, although there are some cross-links, for example in the described order of creation. Nor shall I be discussing *creatio ex nihilo*, creation out of nothing, neither the scientific work nor the recent excitement over the possibility of life on Mars! It is worth noting, however, that recent discoveries have pushed back the first chemical traces of life to more than 3.8 billion years ago, on an earth 4.5 billion years old, and immediately following a late heavy bombardment by meteorites, which is documented in the lunar record.[1] However, we still know very little about the physical and chemical processes that were necessary for the formation of the first, simplest self-replicating system, and this major discontinuity is outside the scope of the theory of evolution.

But what do I mean by evolution? Evolution has been used to describe many things. We speak about the evolution of ideas, of political parties, of morals, of psychosocial evolution, of the evolution of the European Union, and so on. That is, we use the word to describe change, and change for the better. I shall not be using it in this broad sense. By evolution I shall mean *descent with modification*. Descent implies new generations – and hence the nature of inheritance becomes of central importance – and modification implies change. The central idea of evolution is that although many such changes occur all the time, only those changes that enable a particular organism to deal more effectively with its current or new, changed environment – including its predators – will be selected. Thus the first requirement is *variation*; change must be possible and occur. *Overproduction* of the offspring is also necessary for evolution to work – an idea due to Malthus, Erasmus Darwin and Charles Darwin – so that selection is possible and the species survives. This process was called 'natural selection' by Darwin. Later Huxley called the process 'the survival of the fittest' and this phrase has stuck. So the modified organism is better fitted for the new environment, and this is where the idea of improvement has come from. There is no suggestion, anywhere in biology, that this better adaptation to a new environment has anything to do with morals, and in no way does the theory of evolution suggest that the world is getting better. Thus the word is widely misused.

The idea of continuous change is undoubtedly central, and it is important to understand how deeply this affects the way biologists think. The biological world is not fixed in any way; but is always in flux. The genetic material is continuously changing, or being exchanged from one species to another – for example in the soil bacteria. It is plastic, not fixed. For that matter, the physical world is changing too – we are all now familiar with the idea of climate change. The idea of species is undoubtedly an important one – and I shall be returning later to the issues over their origin and maintenance, but biologists do not think of species as being fixed from the time of creation for all time; which was, historically, the simplest way to read the Genesis account. But surely not the only way? I shall argue that a different reading of the Genesis account is an example of the way in which new knowledge, won through the use of our God-given intelligence, has moved us from one interpretation to another.

There is no doubt that the theory of evolution has been one of the major driving ideas of the twentieth century, and is better called a paradigm than a theory. A paradigm is perhaps best described as a new mind set, a new way of looking at the world, and the change in attitudes brought about by the acceptance of the theory of evolution can perhaps only be compared to that brought about by the Newtonian Revolution in the seventeenth century. The idea of change was not of course new; the acceptance of the modern theories of the formation of the rocks over long periods, involving both gradual and catastrophic change, earlier in the century, had seen to that.

The theory of evolution also implied, although it did not prove, that there was a single origin for all living creatures; a single mechanism provided an explanation for the appearance, and disappearance, of all the teeming millions of creatures, past and present, and for their continuing adaptation to changing environments. No wonder it seized the Victorians by the ears! Christians and Jews have, of course, no difficulty with a single origin for all living creatures; it is implied, if not stated explicitly, by the Genesis account.

The theologians and clergy of the mid-nineteenth century were, by and large, accustomed to an old world, and a world of much change. Indeed I understand that none of the clergy of that time, many of whom were evangelicals, believed in the creation of the earth in seven days in 4004 BC. How ironic it is that such a belief is much more common today than it was years ago! In parenthesis, I wondered if you had realized that we have recently passed the 6000th anniversary of the date of the creation as calculated by Bishop Ussher.

So why the great conflict? Why is the theory of evolution seen as *the* great challenge to the Victorian Church, a major defeat in the battle with secularism? We all remember the accounts of that debate in Oxford; Huxley's cutting attack on Bishop Wilberforce, and how the Church retired to lick its wounds. The answer is clear: the theory of evolution was presented as an *alternative* to the biblical account. You chose one or the other, and for the up-to-date Victorian man or woman, surely the new, the scientific explanation was to be preferred to the old, almost medieval explanation? I understand, and this is not my area, that conflict was not the original reaction, but a view propagated later by Huxley, although it has come to be the accepted popular view of the Victorian scene. The conflict is still with us, and I shall return to this point later, but Professor Colin Russell and others have maintained that such conflict was manufactured and unnecessary.[2] I shall propose that we see creation and evolution as complementary rather than being in conflict, although I shall also be describing the two parties in the present conflict.

Darwin first proposed his theory in 1859, before the mechanism of inheritance and the nature of the genetic material was known. It was some years later (1865) that Mendel carried out his simple but profoundly important experiments on the mechanism of inheritance, showing that genetic characteristics were inherited independently, and that reassortment of such characters from two distinguishable but related parents led to a new genetic composition and new observable characteristics. These characters were later called genes, and it was gradually realized that the genetic material of all living organisms was made up of a linear array of such genes. Since all living creatures were constructed in the same way, it did not matter which organism was studied; what was true for one was true for all. Studies on the fruit fly in the early years of the twentieth century then established that such genes could suffer a permanent, heriditable change as a result of exposure to X-rays or to certain chemicals, called mutagens. Here was a mechanism to explain how the genetic material could be changed. Was this the way that evolution had worked? Could it explain the small scale changes and also the big one – particularly the emergence of new species?

For small scale changes *had* been observed. Darwin, in his visit to the Galapagos Islands had been much struck by his famous finches, which differ slightly from island to island. All the finches have rather dull plumage and are very similar except in the size and shape of their beaks. However, they also show important differences: those species that have adapted to seed eating have large, heavy beaks, those that eat insects have small sharp beaks and so on. The finches have evidently evolved into species able to feed on all the types of food available. To quote Charles Darwin, from *The Origin of Species*:

> Seeing this gradation and diversity of structure in one small, intimately related group of birds, one might fancy that from an original paucity of birds in this archipelago, one species has been taken and modified for different end.

A more recent, widely known example is that of the peppered moth. In the industrial regions of England there had been an increase in the frequency of a black, mutant form of this moth, which is better camouflaged against its predators than the normal pale form. With the introduction of the Clean Air Act, the lighter forms have made a comeback in some areas. Evidently, selection can work at this level.

But at more complex levels? Can mutation and selection explain the emergence of completely new species, or the development of completely new organs, such as the eye? Organs which are useless until they are fully formed, and which appear to have evolved independently several times? Surely this is the work of the Grand Designer, Paley's watchmaker? So some Christians have argued: evolution can bring about small-scale changes of course, they say, but what about the big changes? That is where God comes in. I think that it is a dangerous argument – this 'God-of-the-gaps' argument. Science has a habit of slowly and surely filling in those gaps, and then God is always on the retreat. We get nowhere by labelling our ignorance 'God'. We shall have to do better than that.

Molecular Biology

Meantime there has been an explosion of knowledge in the last fifty years in the biological sciences, and some of it certainly bears on the theory of evolution. Fifty years ago, it had just been established that the genetic material was nucleic acid and not protein. There are two sorts of nucleic acid: ribonucleic acid (RNA) and deoxyribonucleic acid (DNA). Both exist in cells as very long molecules and they may be likened to long necklaces, each made up of four different coloured beads. There are many thousands of such beads in any molecule of either RNA or DNA, *and the sequence of the beads is specific and determines the function of the nucleic acid*. The DNA is in the nucleus of the cell, in the form of large complex structures called chromosomes, and is responsible for the faithful carrying of the genetic information from generation to generation. The specific DNA sequence of each gene is then copied into a single strand of RNA, which then transfers the genetic information, which has been encoded in the DNA sequence, from the cell nucleus to the cytoplasm of the cell. Here the code written in the RNA sequence is translated into a third specific sequence in another large class of big molecules called proteins. It is proteins, and many thousands of different proteins are found in any one cell, that are responsible for carrying out the multiple functions necessary for the life of the cell. These proteins may be structural, that is, responsible for the shape and movement of the cell, they may be biological catalysts called enzymes or they may be regulators, controlling the many thousands of chemical reactions that run all the time in any living cell. Biological information, in the form of coded specific sequences, flows from the nucleus, where it is faithfully maintained from generation to generation, to the cytoplasm, where most of the action takes place. This has been neatly expressed in the central dogma of molecular biology: 'DNA makes RNA and RNA makes protein.' It is also evident that not all cells in any particular organism are the same; they may well look different and they will certainly have different functions. It is important to realize however that these differentiated cells all *contain exactly the same DNA*. That is, every cell in my body contains the same DNA; or to put it another way, the total genetic information – all that is needed to totally specify the organism – is present in every cell. However, the DNA functions differently in these different cells. So there have to be switching systems, responsible for differentiation.

Scientists in Cambridge have played a central role in unravelling these relationships. The structure of DNA was proposed by Jim Watson and Francis Crick in a letter to the journal *Nature* in July 1953.[3] This was the famous double helix; and a golden helix can still be seen hanging outside Crick's former home in Portugal Place, Cambridge. The letter ends with a now famous sentence: 'It has not escaped our notice that the specific pairing we have postulated immediately suggests a possible copying mechanism for the genetic material.' It did indeed! The mechanism they had in mind; the separation of the double helix into its two, complementary strands, each of which then acted as a template for the synthesis of two new strands has proved to be correct.

Then Fred Sanger, working in the Medical Research Council Laboratory of Molecular Biology in Cambridge, worked out a way of determining the sequence of a protein, the first being insulin, and then subsequently of DNA. For this outstanding work he received two Nobel prizes. The first three-dimensional structure of two related proteins, myoglobin and globin, was worked out by John Kendrew and by Max Perutz, and later the structure of the nucleosome, the basic building block of the chromosome, was worked out by Aaron Klug, all working at the MRC Laboratory. All three received Nobel prizes. The nature of the genetic code was also worked out during the same period in the 1960s, largely elsewhere, but with important contributions from Francis Crick.

So to sum up the new information:

- the genetic material is made up of a linear array of genes, arranged on one or more chromosomes;
- living organisms contain from 5 or 6 genes in the small viruses to 100,000 in the human;
- genes are precisely duplicated at cell division by separation of the two strands of the double helix and formation of two new daughter strands using the separated strands as templates;
- genes consist of a unique DNA sequence – normally from 600 to 3,000 units long;
- these sequences consist of both coding regions – the sequence that is directly translated into a protein sequence – and non-coding regions that contain various switching systems;
- the genetic code is effectively universal;
- proteins formed through the intermediary role of RNA may be either structural, catalytic or regulatory proteins – including the control of differentiation.

Through the work of Fred Sanger and others it has now become a complex but routine procedure to determine the sequence of a very large number of both proteins and nucleic acids. It then became possible to compare the sequences of two species that show obvious superficial similarities, humans and chimpanzees. The sequences turn out to be astonishingly similar; a number of proteins have identical sequences, and the difference is normally less than 1 per cent. Similar results are obtained by comparison of the nucleic acid sequences; these are more different from each other than are the protein sequences, and for two reasons. The first is that there is more difference in the DNA sequences of the regions *between* the genes than inside them, in regions that are not involved in determining protein sequences; and the second is that the changes are mainly in the third unit of the codon (the three unit group of the DNA sequence that determines a single unit of the protein sequence). Alteration at this particular position has however no effect on the protein sequence, because of what is known as the degeneracy of the code. In other words, change is possible, but does not often take place if it would lead to a change in protein sequence, and thus in function.

What happens when we compare protein sequences of more

different species? There is a mass of data available, and I will restrict myself to that for cytochrome C, a small protein (104 units long) that plays an essential role in metabolism. Determination of the sequences of a large number of species shows that the more different any two species are, the more different are their cytochromes. There are also similarities, the mammals are more similar to each other than the mammals are to the birds or to the reptiles. But even simple yeast shows some similarities to higher animals! I think that the suggestion that these differences arose by changes accompanying evolutionary change from a single ancestral form is much the simplest explanation.

The sequences can be used in another way, to yield more precise estimates of the closeness of the relationships. This comparison can be done with a computer, which compares the differences between different proteins and different DNAs, and then constructs a hypothetical ancestral sequence from which these similar sequences could have been derived. Such an ancestral sequence can then be compared with that derived from another group of organisms, to produce another hypothetical sequence, as an ancestor to them both. This process can be continued to produce an evolutionary tree, in which species are joined by lines which show how much structural relationship exists, while the length of the lines shows how close or how distant is the relationship: the longer the line the more distant the relationship. The striking outcome is that the relationships that result are remarkably similar to those arrived at by classical taxonomy. The construction of the relationship trees makes no assumptions about biological relatedness, but produces an evolutionary picture very similar to that derived from classical biology.

If the distances between different groups depict relatedness, and if it is assumed that there is a constant rate of change in the protein sequences, then the distances are measures of the time taken for an evolutionary change to take place. The time should be measured in generations rather than in years, since what is important is any change in the DNA that is passed on to the next generation, and these changes must take place before production of the next generation. When this is done, the results indicate how long ago the two species diverged, and this can then be compared with the 'classical' dates derived from the interpretation of the fossil record. The results show that different proteins seem to change at different rates, so that the method cannot be used as a precise 'molecular clock' to date evolutionary change, but it does give a picture that is broadly consistent with the picture that is emerging from the fossil record. That is, species which are distantly related on the evolutionary tree generated by the computer diverged a long time ago as judged by the fossil record. Thus two very different and independent approaches give a consistent picture of their evolutionary relationship; surely both must be broadly correct.

However, this approach says nothing about speciation, the production of new non-interbreeding species. There is still much here that we do not understand, but the last few years have seen an explosion in our knowledge of regulatory genes, and in particular the genes that control differentiation. We know now that many of the genes that characterize cancer cells are control genes that have gone wrong. We also know something about the genes that control differentiation – for example, the genes controlling segmentation in insects. It turns out that these are astonishingly similar to differentiation genes in other species, so whatever the mechanism of speciation, different species are built to a common pattern. 'Remarkably, many of the genes that are important for the control of fly development are also crucial players in vertebrate, and by association human, development.'[4] For example, there exists a mouse gene that rejoices in the name of *Sonic hedgehog* (geneticists have a curious sense of humour), which is closely related to a fruit-fly gene called *hedgehog*.[5] In the fruit-fly a mutation in this gene wrecks the development of fly embryos and causes them to assume rounded bristled shapes somewhat reminiscent of a curled-up hedgehog. In the mouse, the gene guides the development of unformed tissue into skin, ribs and backbone. It also stimulates the formation of nerve cells and support cells for the embryonic spinal chord, and it guides the development of the mouse embryo's hands and feet, distinguishing clearly between the different sorts of finger and toe. I do not think that we know how the gene product works, though it is probably through the production of a diffusible substance, which has differing effects depending on its concentration. This is control of differentiation not of speciation, but it must be a first step in understanding speciation, and there is much contemporary interest in identifying genes involved in speciation. As always the scientific explanation grows in its scope, and the space for the 'God-of-the-gaps' shrinks. Not a happy position to hold. I used to wonder whether we would need a new paradigm to explain speciation. I think that that is increasingly unlikely, and the explanation will come from the 'normal' linear increase in scientific knowledge; maybe in my lifetime.

The fact remains that evolution is still a theory. and how can one ever prove or disprove such a theory? The course of evolution cannot be rerun! But that is not how such theories, locked into historical and prehistorical time, can be tested. They are tested over and over again, by every scientific investigation, and a single discovery, for example the discovery of human remains (a skull say) in Pre-Cambrian strata or, less fancifully, contemporary with the dinosaurs, would blow it sky-high. What a prize that would be, but no one has found it! The evidence is cumulative and massive, and I am fully persuaded.

Creationism

But not everyone is persuaded, and a substantial group of Christians, who call themselves Creationists or Creation Scientists, reject the theory of evolution in favour of what they regard as the true teaching of the Bible. They are in a particularly strong position in the United States, where they have succeeded in having 'Creation Science' established as needing to be taught as an alternative to the theory of evolution in the schools in the US South and California. They are particularly strong in the Southern Baptists and a number of allied denominations, and they are fundamentalist in doctrine. They are not so strong in Britain, but have a number of established speakers, and many biology teachers in universities will have had the experience of having a first-year biology student announce at the beginning of the course that he or she does not believe in evolution.

I must say that I think that it is extremely regrettable that any group of Christians should take to themselves a title that implies that those Christians who do not agree with them do not believe that God created the Earth and all that it contains. The Creationists see the theory of evolution as an attempt to provide an entirely naturalistic explanation for the origin of the universe and all it contains, and there is no doubt that in some hands it is just that, a point that I will return to later. However, I do not think that this excuses their attitude to other Christians, with whom they do not agree. But I am afraid that Christendom has always been 'blessed' with exclusive groups. The position of some of their spokesmen is quite extreme. For example, Henry Morris has written that: 'One can be a Christian and an evolutionist just as one can be a Christian thief, or a Christian adulterer, or a Christian liar. It is absolutely impossible for those who profess to believe the Bible and to follow Christ to embrace evolutionism.'[6] No wonder ordinary churchgoers in some American denominations feel the pressure to fall into line!

Creationists maintain that 'the world as we know it is 10,000 years old; dinosaurs lived at the same time as man and they were wiped out by the Flood' to quote Robert Simonds,[7] president of the National Association of Christian Educators, a body that claims to represent 350,000 parents of American schoolchildren. Creationists also maintain that the theory of evolution is just that; no more than a theory which has never been proved, and which has numerous inconsistencies and failures, which the scientific establishment has covered up. To quote D. T. Gish, one of their leading spokesmen:

> No scientist would ever be rewarded with a Nobel Prize for replacing Darwinian evolution with creation. In the first place, his publication would most likely never see the light of day, certainly not in standard science journals, and secondly he would be ostracised by the so-called scientific community for suggesting creation as an alternative to evolution.[8]

Note how creation and evolution are set up as mutually exclusive alternatives; this is a conflict situation.

What is the Creationist position? First, that the world is not very old, but was created over the seven days of Genesis chapter one. They see any other view as being disloyal to the authority of Genesis and to the fourth Commandment (in six days . . .). By implication, they assume that God's sovereign acts are always sudden rather than through a process. I do not see why this should be so. They reject, or explain away, radiometric dating and deal with the geological evidence for an old earth by postulating a 'mature creation', that is, the earth was created relatively recently (although not in 4004 BC) and rapidly, but with an appearance of age. Alternatively, E. H. Andrews[9] postulates 'miraculous process' in which the normal laws of the natural order (which I think we all accept depend on the upholding power of God) are changed so that processes that normally take a very long time, such as the deposit of sedimentary rocks, take place almost instantaneously. I have to say that

I find this very unconvincing, and hope that I never find myself having to defend my faith with such *ad hoc* arguments.

Second, they deny the theory of evolution, although not the possibility of small-scale changes. To quote D. T. Gish again: 'The claim that God used evolution rather than special creation to bring the universe and the living things it contains into being denies the omniscience and omnipotence of God and makes a mockery of Scripture.'

Gish goes on to argue[10] that:

1 The evolutionary explanation is improbable; mutation and natural selection cannot generate new complexity. At best it is a 'conservative force, weeding out the unfit'. In response R. J. Berry[11] points out that:
  – a small but significant proportion of newly-arisen mutations are advantageous to their carriers;
  – mutations are random in their occurrence, but evolutionary change is directed in its occurrence.

2 Evolution is against the Second Law of Thermodynamics. This is not my area of expertise, but this assertion has been rejected on the grounds that order can arise in a non-equilibrium system.[12] Thermodynamics applies to a *closed* system, but the earth is receiving energy from the sun, and the system is not closed.

3 Evolution demands the formation of transitional forms, which have not been found. However, others have argued that such transitional forms are by definition unstable, and therefore likely to be rare. Time and continued excavation have certainly produced more transitional forms, particularly in the humanoids.

4 In particular, Creationists argue that the Bible insists, and excavation shows that man, and woman in the person of Eve, is a special creation, and not derived by evolution from other species. Personally, I do not consider that the Bible demands such an interpretation, and the archaeological evidence for transitional forms is now formidable and well known.

However, if Christians are prepared to accept that the Genesis account can be read in more than one way (and I am), then the objections to the theory of evolution, although well worth putting as part of the normal debate, are not persuasive. Indeed, many Christians would accept that evolution is part of

God's way of providing for the creation of different species. This is not to say, however, that acceptance of the theory of evolution means that we have to accept that the world, and all that is in it, is without purpose or design, a view that inevitably leads to the deep pessimism well expressed by Monod in his book *Chance and Necessity*.[13]

Richard Dawkins

However there are those who say exactly that; the world we know through science is all that there is, and that we dangerously delude ourselves if we think otherwise. The prophet of this message is Richard Dawkins, until recently Reader in Zoology in the University of Oxford, and now Professor of the Public Understanding of Science in the same university. He has a high reputation in the field of ethology, and has written a number of books and articles on evolutionary biology, of which the most recent is *Climbing Mount Improbable*.[14] He is well known to the public from a number of television appearances, is very intelligent, highly articulate and persuasive, and preaches his gospel with almost evangelical zeal.

Professor Dawkins relentlessly advocates the conflict thesis, and in doing so, is dismissive of theology, as summarized in 'The Poole-Dawkins Debate'.[15] *Inter alia* he states:

> What has 'theology' ever said that is of the smallest use to anybody? When has 'theology' ever said anything that is demonstrably true and is not obvious? . . . What makes you think that 'theology' is a subject at all?

He also contends that religion is a scientific theory:

> Until recently one of religion's main functions was scientific; the explanation of existence, of the universe, of life . . . So the most basic claims of religion are scientific. Religion is a scientific theory.

So Dawkins sees the 'hypothesis of God' as an explanatory hypothesis which is in competition with evolution by natural selection: 'God and natural selection are, after all, the only two workable theories of why we exist.' Dawkins contends that the idea of God is intrinsically improbable and over complex. 'Who designed the divine creator?' is a repeated question. So God is no more than one more link in the causal chain, not different in kind from any other link in the chain. Supernatural events are no different from improbable events, 'faith is the great cop-out, the great excuse to evade the need to think and evaluate evidence'. Religious faith, unlike scientific faith is unevidenced belief, because only scientific evidence is trustworthy evidence. Inevitably he rejects any argument from design; he asserts that the world only admits of physical explanations, not being aware that a description of the processes does not eliminate any idea of a divine agency. So the title of perhaps his most influential book is *The Blind Watchmaker*,[16] a reference, of course, to Paley. There, and in an earlier book, he uses his memorable phrase 'the selfish gene', meaning, I think, self-preserving in the long-run, but using a word that has another meaning usually associated with behaviour and morality. This leads to a new proposal, the 'meme', which he describes thus:

> I think that a new kind of replicator has recently emerged on this very planet...but already it is achieving evolutionary change at a rate that leaves the old gene panting far behind.

Examples of memes are tunes, ideas, catch-phrases, clothes fashions, and so forth, and the ideas of God, of hell-fire and faith. But of course *disbelief* in these ideas could also be due to a meme. The argument is double-edged, and all he is really saying is that there is a current of ideas. So what is new? His total rationalism inevitably leads him to reject any idea of purpose, other than scientific. His view is very clearly expressed in the following passages:

> [after a little girl of six pointed out some flowers] I asked her what she thought flowers were for? She gave a very thought-ful answer. 'Two things' she said; 'to make the world pretty and to help the bees make honey for us'. Well, I thought that was a very nice answer and I was very sorry that I had to tell her that it wasn't true. Her answer was not too different from the answer that most people throughout history would have given. The very first chapter of the Bible sets it out. Man has dominion over all living things. The animals and the plants were there for our benefit.

and he continues:

> We are machines built by DNA whose purpose is to make more copies of the same DNA...Flowers are for the same thing as everything else in the living kingdoms, for spreading

'copy-me' programmes about, written in DNA language . . .
This is EXACTLY what we are for. We are machines for prop-
agating DNA, and the propagation of DNA is a self-sustaining
process. It is every object's sole object for living . . .

This is the gospel according to Dawkins.

I find some of this poignant, some saddening; is there really
so little to life? Much of it strikes me as arrogant. Is there nothing that men and women down the ages have learnt that is
worth retaining? And as for music, art, literature, aesthetics,
they seem to have no place in his world. It is a logically-consis-
tent, well-articulated rationalistic world-view, which is clearly in
conflict with any religious view, and must be answered. Much of
Dawkins' world-view depends on his central thesis that 'religion
is a scientific theory' including his view of 'God as a competing
explanation [to science] for facts about the universe and life'. I
do not think that any professional philosopher, and certainly
not Professor Mary Hesse, who writes on this issue later in this
volume, would make such a claim, and conspicuous by its
absence, is any attempt by Dawkins to justify such a contentious
claim. It is a supreme example of what the late Donald MacKay
called 'nothing-buttery thinking'. This chapter could correctly
be described as 'nothing but' black marks on white paper. I
hope that it is more than that.

Resolution

Now it is time to turn from analysis to synthesis. To turn from
monolithic, conflictual views of the world to resolution. To look
for complementary explanations. Many have pointed out that
there are a number of different types of explanation. For
example, a thermostat might be described as:

- a device for maintaining a constant temperature (an inter-
  pretative explanation);
- a device that consists of a bi-metallic strip in close prox-
  imity to an electrical contact (a descriptive explanation);
- a device that maintains a constant temperature because,
  when the temperature falls, the bi-metallic strip bends,
  so making electrical contact. It switches on a heater which
  operates until, at a certain temperature, the strip bends
  away from the contact, thereby breaking the circuit (a scientific explanation).[17]

These three explanations are *not* in conflict; but are completely *compatible*. Or, to use a well-known illustration of Donald MacKay's: you go into the kitchen at home to find the kettle boiling on the stove. You ask:

'Why is the kettle boiling?'

and your colleague, who is taking an Open University course, replies:

'Because the vapour pressure is equal to atmospheric pressure.'

You are interested, and ask;

'Why is the vapour pressure that high?'

and the reply comes quickly:

'Because kinetic energy has been imparted to the water molecules by the exothermic oxidation of methane in the coal gas'

and you might, or might not perhaps, ask about the thermodynamics of the oxidation reaction, and so on.

However you might get a quite different answer to your original question:

'Because I want a cup of tea!'

Two different answers to what is apparently the same question. One giving a series of explanations, one after the other, each answer provoking another question, in what is called a causal chain; the other involving purpose and choice. The first question is the sort we ask as scientists; they are really 'How?' questions. The second is a real 'Why?' question, and we do ask those questions about our own lives, about their purpose, for example. It is these questions that Dawkins denies have any validity and to which Christianity, among others, offers answers.

So I contend that indeed there is more than one type of question that can be asked, and in this way we can avoid the conflict situation, inevitably adversarial, and look for complementary explanations in which science asks broadly 'How?' questions and religion 'Why?' questions. But how do they fit together? We have to be careful not to appear to hold two positions that do not conflict only because they do not intersect, a world-view where God's activity is so carefully hidden as to be undetectable. That would make our position intellectually unassailable but irrelevant to those who believe in the efficiency of science to explain all that there is. So although this idea of complementarity is useful, especially in ground-clearing, we might need to give more thought to how far it is applicable. Are all accounts only complementary to another account? Surely the Judaeo-Christian view of the world was an important element in the development of the scientific method? So do not the accounts overlap here?

So are there connections between the scientific and religious accounts of our world, and particularly about the origin of life and its diversity? There is certainly no obvious conflict between the essential message of Genesis chapter one and our current scientific understanding. But is there no evidence for design in the biological world? Recently, there has been a revival of interest in the argument from design in cosmology, as described by John Polkinghorne in Chapter Two. The balance between the different physical constants is so fine and the probability of forming a stable universe with its range of chemical elements is so low that the argument for a Designer takes on a new force. There is nothing comparable in biology, and the arguments that have been put forward for design[18] have not convinced reviewers, and sound suspiciously like the 'God-of-the-gaps' approach.

Oliver Barclay[19] has pointed out that the New Testament does not use the modern form of design arguments. It appeals rather to our awareness of the Creator from looking at the natural world and 'seeing' how marvellously *the whole thing works* and, amazingly, makes human life possible and pleasant. It is more an argument from aesthetic awareness than a logical argument, but it affects us all nevertheless. I suggest that we are on much surer ground when we consider those occasions when God intervened in the natural world, for example, in the resurrection. While such accounts have been somewhat of an embarrassment to a few Christians, these 'mighty acts of God' are both the assurance of our own faith and our rebuttal to those who contend that science explains all that there is. It is also the case for moving from God as 'The Grand Designer of the Universe' to the God of the New Testament. We must never be ashamed of the Supernatural breaking in.

Chapter Five

BRAIN, MIND AND SOUL

Fraser Watts

T hough it was cosmology that first raised issues about the compatibility of science and religious belief, it is the human sciences that have come to present an increasingly strong challenge to religious belief. At several points in the human sciences, there are strong 'nothing but' ideologies about human nature that are not easily reconciled with a religious view of human beings. These are the views that we are nothing but survival machines for our genes, have minds that are nothing but computer programmes, that we are nothing but our nervous systems, and so on.

I call these views 'ideologies' because I do not think they are inherently scientific. They are not scientific in the sense of being necessary starting assumptions for research programmes in their fields; science does not need to make these assumptions. Neither are they in any way legitimate conclusions from scientific research, there is no actual data that compels such conclusions. Far from being an essential part of the scientific study of human beings, I would submit that these 'nothing but' ideologies are bad science, because they constrain and distort open-minded scientific enquiry.

There is another reason why these 'nothing but' assumptions come into conflict with conventional religious belief, and it is to do with the fact that they are in fact quasi-religious beliefs themselves. They represent religious beliefs that have taken an atheist turn. Deep within science, and going back at least to the seventeenth century, there has been a scientific programme of demystifying the world, stripping the mystery away and exposing nature to the naked eye. (Incidentally, as Mary Midgley has pointed out in *Science as Salvation*,[1] the sexist language about 'stripping away the veil' and so forth in much seventeenth-century writing about science is quite extraordinary.) These 'nothing but' ideologies can be seen as a direct continuation of that programme of demystification. Stripping away the mystery about human beings is, from this point of view, one of the last citadels that has to be stormed.

This programme of demystification has not always been seen as anti-religious. Too strong a sense of mystery about the world was originally seen as antagonistic to orthodox Christianity. Demystification was originally seen as being an ally of orthodox religion against paganism. However, through a curious shifting of alliances during the scientific age, excessive zeal for demystification has now come to be an enemy of religion.

In the light of this programme of demystification, it is no surprise that Dan Dennett at the start of his widely read, but misleadingly entitled, book, *Consciousness Explained*[2] says that consciousness is 'just about the last surviving mystery'. The feeling that we are on the brink of understanding this last, central mystery about ourselves generates much excitement. In another recent book on human consciousness, Owen Flanagan says that 'understanding consciousness with the conscious mind is a wonderful giddy idea'.[3]

It is worth pausing for a moment to try to catch the overtones of this excitement, to try to grasp why people are so deeply stirred by it. In part, of course, it is simply the excitement of beginning to make progress with a really difficult scientific project. However, I sense that there is something deeper, some strange inarticulate idea that perhaps if we understood ourselves we would be like gods. There is a kind of daring in seeking such knowledge, in no longer accepting that understanding consciousness is, in the words of Psalm 139, 'too wonderful and excellent for me'. It is like eating the forbidden fruit. Understanding human consciousness has become, in some ways, the modern equivalent of eating the fruit of the tree of knowledge of good and evil.

Consciousness is currently the focus of enormous scientific interest. But it is of *religious interest* too. Let me briefly set out some of the key reasons why mind and consciousness might be important from a religious point of view. Consciousness is perhaps the most important flowering of creation within our remarkable human race. We seem to have a special kind of consciousness, manifested particularly in language and in our unique capacity to reflect on what we know. That in turn gives us a capacity for judgement, discernment and freedom not found elsewhere in creation. It is, in effect, with human consciousness that creation has become spiritual.

Consciousness is also very important in the spiritual life. There is a particular kind of consciousness involved in spirituality. It is through our consciousness that we come to have an awareness of God, or divinity. The religious life is founded upon a religious way of interpreting the world, making sense of it, seeing it shot through with manifestations of God. Becoming religious involves a new and changed consciousness. The *metanoia* of which the Christian tradition speaks, usually translated 'repentance', is more literally a new consciousness.

Sometimes, this religious interest in consciousness is pushed unhelpfully far. One idea, touted in some philosophical circles, concerns the link between God and consciousness. Some people think that God can be thought about as a kind of mind, in some sense analogous to the human mind, or as some sort of disembodied centre of consciousness.[4] Though this has become an important part of how we think about God, I want to urge caution about it. All thinking about God is of course analogical, and none of it can be pressed too far without becoming seriously misleading. At the beginning of the scientific age, rather surprisingly, people came to think much more readily than in previous centuries about the mind existing separately from the body. This is not really a traditional part of biblical thinking or of Christian belief. It is problematic from many points of view to think about human beings as an assembly of distinct minds and bodies, and it is unsatisfactory to base our thinking about God on such an inherently problematic analogy.

Brain and Mind

There is nothing in the specifically religious emphasis on consciousness as a spiritual property of human beings that in any way denies its grounding in the natural, material world. I am not remotely uncomfortable with the Darwinian insight that we have evolved from simpler creatures in the natural world. On the contrary, I welcome it, because it emphasizes that we are natural as well as spiritual creatures. In human beings, the natural and spiritual come together. We are, in that sense, the 'hinge' of creation. (I would prefer incidentally, to talk about us in that way that in the more usual terms of the 'crown' of creation. That seems to be claiming rather too much for us; we are certainly not perfect, perhaps not even final.)

Wanting, as I do, to emphasize the grounding of consciousness in the natural world, I also see nothing problematic, from a religious point of view, in the modern scientific interest in discovering how consciousness arises within the brain. Most scientists assume that consciousness is some kind of emergent property of the brain, and so do I. There seems no other plausible possibility. I certainly do not want to argue as some philosophers such as John Locke have done, that consciousness has no natural explanation, so it must be the direct endowment of a divine being.

There is currently much interest in the so-called 'hard' question of how the brain gives rise to our distinctive human form of consciousness. This seems to me a wholly sensible and valid scientific question. Not much definite progress has so far been made, though there are interesting leads and speculations. There is no need to go into these here. Neither am I going to get deeply into the quagmire of current philosophy of mind, except to say that I assume that we need a position that holds together two common sense points.

One is that mind and consciousness are real, distinct and novel properties. There is no future in wishing them away, or in arguing that there is nothing to be explained. The second basic assumption is that these properties are grounded in the physical brain. There is again no future in the idea that they have come from nowhere, or directly from God, like a meteorite from outer space. Within those basic points there is much middle ground to be explored, and I am happy to leave the details to the philosophers.

Reductionism

The trouble comes from a tendency in some circles to talk about consciousness in provocative 'nothing but' terms. A recent example that gained a good deal of publicity was Francis Crick's claim in his book, *The Astonishing Hypothesis: The Scientific Search for the Soul*[5] that we are 'nothing more than a bundle of neurones'. Either that means that there is no such thing as consciousness to be explained, which to my mind flies in the face of common sense. Or it means that we can give such a complete account of consciousness, in terms of the brain processes in which it is grounded, that it is really redundant to speak of higher human properties such as consciousness at all. We could, in the jargon, 'reduce' all talk about mind, consciousness or soul, to neurological terms.[6]

This seems to be going much too far, and to be much too dogmatic. By all means let us try as best we can to explain consciousness in terms of the brain. I assume that we will eventually make a good deal of progress. There is increasing evidence for what has been called a 'tightening' of the mind–brain link.[7] We have identified brain cells with highly specific functions, for example cells specialized for the recognition of faces, even different cells for recognizing people face-on from the ones involved in recognizing them in profile. Much more such knowledge will accumulate. Further, I guess that we will develop a scientific story about what type of brain activity underpins higher forms of consciousness.

But we do not know how far we will get. Never in science, as far as I know, has it been possible to give a complete explanation of one thing in terms of another, and I do not see any reason why this should be the first exception. When new properties emerge, new laws tend to emerge as well. Higher processes, though grounded in lower level ones, tend to manifest properties that are not wholly explicable in terms of lower level properties, and laws that are not mere reflections of lower activity. I anticipate that there will be laws about consciousness that we will not be able to recast completely as laws about the brain.

Anyhow, I am content to approach these matters on an experimental basis. Let us see how far we get. What I find puzzling, and contrary to the spirit of science, is the dogmatic assertion, ahead of time, that the explanation of consciousness in terms of the brain will be completely successful, and that therefore it can already be claimed that we are nothing more than a bundle of neurones.

Artificial Intelligence

There are exactly parallel points to be made about Artificial Intelligence (AI), the enterprise of developing programmes that will enable computers to simulate human intelligence.[8] This is an enterprise in which real progress has been made. For example, the program 'Deep Blue' has beaten the world champion Kasparov at chess. AI is an enterprise which has a considerable range of valuable technological applications. Also, from the point of view of pure science, there is much value in trying to cast theories about how the human mind works in terms of a computer program. It is a language which is helpfully precise, and will, I believe, prove as valuable in psychology as mathematics has been in physics. For these various reasons, AI is a worthwhile scientific enterprise.

What causes trouble, again, is the dogmatic assertion, ahead of time, that the AI project will be completely successful, that in twenty or thirty years we will have computers that can simulate all intelligent human activities. An interesting example arose in some correspondence between Edward Furse and myself in *The Tablet* in which he claimed that, because prayer is an intelligent activity, it would soon be possible to program computers to pray.[9]

What is, of course, correct is that any rule-based mental activity can be programmed into a computer. The question is how far prayer can be reduced to a rule-based activity. Certainly, there are elements that are based on implicit rules, rules about when particular types of prayer are appropriate, and rules about how to construct them. What is problematic is the claim that there is nothing more to prayer than following such implicit rules. Even if a computer were following the same rules, it is a huge leap to claim that it would in every sense be praying in the same way as a human being, having the same spiritual relationship to God, and so on. There is no basis in science for such a claim.

Complementarity of Mind and Brain

However, let us return from Artificial Intelligence to issues about mind and brain. If, as I assume, mind and consciousness are grounded in the brain, there is a question about what relationship there is between what we can cryptically call 'mind-talk' and 'brain-talk'. It is possible, at least in principle, to describe what is on someone's mind, that is, to describe their 'mind-state', as it is sometimes called. It is also possible in principle to describe their brain-state. Moreover, given that mind is grounded in the brain, there is bound to be a close link between the two. The key question is how close the link is. Some people are arguing that the link is so close that mind-talk is redundant, and is just a folksy way of saying what could be said more exactly in terms of the brain. It is a view that goes under the name of eliminative materialism, because it is a materialistic position, emphasizing the 'matter' of the brain, and regarding mind-talk as eliminable.

Like a lot of problematic claims in this area, it is at best highly speculative. Certainly, it has not been established scientifically that there is the kind of exact one-to-one mapping between mind and brain that is sometimes claimed. Indeed, it is hardly conceivable that such evidence could be produced at present. We are simply not in a position to give the kind of complete and exact description of mind-states and brain-states that would be required. Philosophers have an unsatisfactory way of talking glibly about states of mind and brain, glossing over the fact that we are not able to actually describe them, except in the most sketchy way.

I can make all this a bit more concrete by referring to one of the research interests I had in my scientific days, which was to do with going to sleep. You can give at least an approximate description of going to sleep in terms of the mental changes involved; your thought processes get increasingly fragmentary, less controlled, perhaps a little bizarre, as you approach sleep. At the same time, the electrical rhythms of the brain get slower and larger as sleep approaches. Now there is a rough mapping of one set of changes onto the other, though, as far as we can see, it is only rough; there doe not seem to be an exact correspondence. But even if there were, the two aspects of going to sleep are just different; it is hard to see that either description of what is involved in going to sleep could be regarded as redundant. The view that mind-talk is, in principle, eliminable thus seems highly implausible.

There is a related tendency in some circles to assume that it makes no real difference whether we actually become conscious of something or not. It is sometimes supposed that all necessary 'information processing' is carried on at a tacit level. This view gains its attractiveness from attempts to model how the mind works in terms of a computer program. Because computers cannot have consciousness, it is attractive for those strongly committed to AI to believe that consciousness is unimportant in human beings too. In fact, of course, it can make a huge difference whether you remember something or not. Remembering a repressed memory of child abuse can change someone's whole outlook. For good empirical reasons, it is essential to retain a language which enables us to discriminate between whether memories or ideas are conscious or not.

Religious and Natural Discourses

One of the theological reasons for being interested in all this is that the issues raised by eliminative materialism are very similar to those raised by atheism. We can talk about what is going on in the world in purely natural terms, making no reference to God, just as we can talk about the brain in purely material terms making no reference to the mind. Alternatively, we can also talk about what is going on in the world in terms of the activity of God, or the movement of the Spirit. I would argue that these two perspectives on the world, the natural on the one hand and the theological or spiritual on the other, are complementary perspectives on the same reality. They describe inherently related things from different points of view, in the same way as our mind- and brain-stories about going to sleep describe the single process of going to sleep from different points of view.

Just as I have argued that we need both mind-stories and brain-stories to describe something such as going to sleep, so I would argue that we need both material and spiritual perspectives on the world. It is inappropriate to try to eliminate one perspective, and to argue that the natural or material perspective is the only valid one. Notice that I am not saying that there is a separate non-material world, comparable to the material one. Minds are not entities in the same sense as brains, even though we undoubtedly have mental properties and powers that cannot be shuffled under the carpet by eliminative materialists. Equally, I am not necessarily arguing for an immaterial or spiritual world that is separate from the material world. At least as far as we are able to apprehend things, the material and the spiritual domains are inextricably intertwined. They are different aspects of what is, for us, the same reality.

Pressing this a little further, there may be some events in the world that it is particularly important to describe from a religious point of view. There are mental events, such as recovering a repressed memory of abuse as a child, that it is especially important to describe in mental terms, if we are to capture the essence of the event. Of course, there could be an account of such an event in brain terms, but it would not adequately capture the essence of its significance. In a similar way, there may be events for which a purely naturalistic account would be particularly inadequate, and a religious account particularly important. Those events that we call 'miracles', or special acts of God's providence, may be such events. I would assume that, like all events, they could be described from both natural and theological points of view. However, the natural account might be conspicuously inadequate in such cases, and the religious account particularly important.

However, the analogy between theological and mental perspectives cannot be pressed all the way. Though I assume that mental powers such as consciousness evolved from a natural basis, I am not necessarily making the comparable claim about the fundamental spiritual reality that we call God. I am assuming that he exists beyond and before the natural world within which we have arisen. Mind can be seen as an emergent property of the natural world, and the *idea* of God might be seen as part of this emergent mental world. However, God himself cannot be seen as an emergent property of the natural world.

Soul and Consciousness

The specifically religious interest in consciousness is mainly in the higher aspects of consciousness that are involved in morality, religious experience and the sense of self. There is not really any agreed term for these in the literature, nor any clear way of formulating them. However, it may be reasonable to refer to them as 'soul-consciousness'.

The best way of making sense of 'soul talk' is to see it as referring to qualitative aspects of people, rather than to some special entity that has a wholly non-natural origin and is in some way implanted by God. The Jungian psychologist James Hillman has been more specific than most about what we mean by soul:

> By soul I mean, first of all, a perspective rather than a substance... This perspective is reflective; it mediates events and makes differences between ourselves and everything that happens... [Soul] is the unknown component that makes meaning possible, turns events into experiences, is communicated in love, and has a religious concern.[10]

There are useful lessons to be learned from how we talk about mind, for how we should talk about soul. As Ryle[11] pointed out, the mind is not a thing in the same sense as the body, but separate from it and additional to it. We do better to say that we have *powers* of mind that arise from our bodies and brains, and which interact with them. It is difficult to find a suitable way of phrasing these points without appearing to imply a greater distinction between mind and brain than is intended. Even to talk about 'strong links' and 'reciprocal effects' may make it sound as though mind and brain are really separate things. Even though mind and brain can be distinguished, they are so closely linked that they cannot really be divided. I believe that this points the way to how we should talk about the human soul. I would not want to say of the soul, any more than of the mind, that it was a thing. The soul is not another entity, separate from the body and the mind, and additional to them. Hillman is surely on the right lines when he says it is a 'perspective' rather than a 'substance'.

But if souls are not separate from our bodies and minds, how do they relate to them? If we were trying to capture a complete human personality in computer terms, I would not want to include a module called the 'soul' along with modules dealing with various other faculties. Neither would I want to have it as a kind of homunculus in the centre of the mind, monitoring and controlling everything that was going on. Rather, I would see 'soul' as an emergent property of the whole system. The recent trend towards modelling the mind as a distributed system may eventually be helpful here. It will lead us to see various mental and emotional properties as emergent properties of a distributed system. I believe that this is the direction in which we should eventually look for thinking scientifically about how properties of soul arise within people.

Yet that is not all we would want to say about the soul. Theologically, as Ward[12] has argued, there are important *both/and* things to be said about soul. It is partly natural, but partly supernatural. It is partly facing towards our human nature, but partly facing towards God, bestowed by him and open to him in a special way. Most important of all, talk about the soul has involved an assertion that there is an openness to God in each person, and that there is potential in each of us to draw closer to God. This seems to lead on to a qualitative use of the concept of soul; some people have more depth of soul than others. Even here I do not think it is necessary to say that people have a soul, as a separate kind of thing, in addition to the bodies and minds that they also have.

Talking about the soul has also been a way of saying that there is a capacity for eternal life in each person. We need to be careful here because there is a lot of confusion in the public mind about what Christian beliefs are; it is not that each one of us survives after death simply by virtue of having a soul. It is not enough to simply *have* a soul. Rather it is a matter of the extent to which each person, through openness to God, has developed the qualities of soul that can be called 'eternal life'. Christians see eternal life as arising from our participation in the eternity of God, rather than from anything inherent in human beings. We also need to be wary of the idea that life beyond death is survival of a thing called the soul that has become totally independent of the body. Christians have traditionally looked for eternal life as whole people, body, mind and spirit, yet transformed in some way that is beyond our current comprehension.

Religious Experience

Lastly, let me come to religious experience, and raise a number of questions that can usefully be approached in the light of the general position I have set out so far.

There is often a tendency to argue that at least some religious experience is 'unmediated'.[13] We need to be wary of that way of talking because, if used loosely, it can be taken to imply that religious experience is somehow independent of the natural and social worlds. However, we should remember that, even in religious experience, we do not cease to be natural beings. Religious experience, like all experience, is grounded in the brain and has neurological correlates. Also, religious experience must be formed and moulded by the language and categories that we have developed in our ordinary social existence. Surely there could be no experience at all, religious or otherwise, that was radically independent of our natural life.

I am equally distrustful of trying to establish whether a particular religious experience is authentic in terms of whether or not it can be understood in natural terms. It is, of course, important to note that the celebrated mystics have generally not been gullible about their experiences. On the contrary, they have sought to discern whether a particular experience should be regarded as authentic or not. That seems to me wholly admirable. Religious gullibility is both pretentious and dangerous. The issue is how one should go about such discernment. The tendency is sometimes to seek to establish authenticity on the basis of a presumed absence of natural explanation. Thus, for example, Ignatius of Loyola looks for what he calls 'uncaused consolation'.[14] (Consolation here means roughly an authentic religious experience.)

I would want to suggest a different approach, arising from what I said earlier about complementary discourses. I have talked about mind and brain discourses being complementary, describing things from different perspectives. By analogy, I suggested that natural and religious discourses were complementary in a similar way, each applicable to any particular event, but capturing different aspects of it. On this basis, I assume that there are no experiences at all, religious or otherwise, that could not be described in natural as well as religious terms. It follows that if the criterion of an authentic religious experience is that no natural account of it is available, there could be no authentic religious experiences at all. Also, it would be very odd theologically to assume that God does not and cannot work through natural processes, though that seems to be implicit in the programme of seeking to establish the authenticity of religious experiences by showing that they cannot be understood in natural terms.

In the following chapter, d'Aquili and Newberg will set out in detail a theory of exactly how the brain gives rise to religious experience, in terms of the operation of what they call the 'causal' and 'holistic' operators. Some people might take that as a complete explanation of religious experience, making it unnecessary to invoke a real God. However, it does not have to be taken in that way. A neurological theory of religious experience can equally well be seen as complementing a religious perspective which assumes the truth and validity of religious experience. On this view, the neurological theory becomes an account of the natural processes by which the real God makes himself known.

Religious Interpretation

The final issue about religions experience that I want to raise, interconnected with the previous one, takes up a vigorous current debate between two quite different theories of religious experience. On one view, religious experience is seen as experience of a wholly distinct realm that we might call the spiritual or the supernatural or, if you prefer, experience of a wholly distinct being that we call God. In recent years an alternative account of religious experience has been strongly canvassed.[15]

This would place the emphasis, not on a distinct realm of experience, but on the application of a religious frame of reference to any experience at all. From this point of view, any experience at all could be 'religious' provided that things were looked at from a religious point of view.

This is, in may ways, an attractive approach. To confine 'religious' experience to a narrow range of unusual experiences marginalizes religion. God becomes confined to a few special moments. Such an approach also comes dangerously close to equating the religious with the inexplicable, with events for which it is difficult to offer a convincing natural account. That, I have already suggested, is the wrong road to go down.

However, there are even more important reasons for not limiting religious experience in this way. It plays down the creative element in religious experience. In very broad terms, I believe there is a story to be told about how religious experience has changed over the last few thousand years. There are good reasons for thinking that religious experience used to be more animistic than is now normally the case. It was apparently commonplace to see the natural world as inhabited by divine beings. Experience of the divine was received relatively passively from the outside world. People heard and saw the gods as part of normal experience.

We have come gradually to find ourselves in a new situation in which religious experience increasingly calls for imaginative powers of perception and discernment. Religious experience is not unique in this. Looking sufficiently carefully at a great painting to see its full significance is dependent on the powers of discernment that we bring. Equally, coming to have a deep level of insight into our own personalities, or those of others, depends on a capacity for discernment that can see below the surface and may have to be cultivated over a long period.

As animistic experience has faded, it seems that religious experience has increasingly come to take the form of seeing the world through creative, religious eyes. Indeed, I see the strengthening of this capacity as being one of the central purposes of the work of Christ. It is, I suggest, one reason why the New Testament has so much to say about the 'sowing' of the word in the soil, which is ourselves, and gift of the Spirit within us. In the Christian age, it seems that religious experience is felt to come increasingly from within rather than from without.[16]

This picks up once again the point about complementary

discourses. Events that are perceived in a religious way are not events that could not be seen in any other way, events for which no natural account was available. Rather, they are events that are seen with spiritual eyes, events that are discerned to some degree in the light of the Spirit.

Conclusion

In this chapter, I have sought to establish an approach to questions about the soul and about religious experience that is firmly based in what we have learned from scientific research and contemporary philosophy about mind being grounded in both the brain and in our social life. I have sought to eschew two extreme positions, one that we are 'nothing but' our physical brains, the other that our mental and 'soul' life can somehow float completely free of our material and social existence. I hope I have shown how it is possible to acknowledge the importance of the material and social basis of our existence, but yet also acknowledge the remarkable properties of mind, and qualities of soul, that human beings have.

Chapter Six

THE NEUROPSYCHOLOGY OF RELIGION

Eugene G. d'Aquili and
Andrew B. Newberg

The definition of the concept of religion is a notoriously difficult task. Many scholars maintain that the concept has no single referent. This is easy to understand since the term 'religion' often encompasses such disparate elements as Eastern monism, Western dualism, divine immanence, divine transcendence, attempts at controlling nature and the environment, achieving and maintaining a plethora of interior states, emphasis on moral behaviour, and so forth. It is difficult to see much in common between the religion of various primitive societies and, say, the exalted spiritual awareness of Theravada Buddhism. Likewise it is often very difficult to see much similarity between practitioners of the same religion. Thus, a behavioural analysis, and to a certain extent a cognitive one, would see very little in common between the Catholicism of a rural South American Indian and that of a Meister Eckhart or of an Anselm of Canterbury. In view of such notable differences, can we hope to arrive at anything like a unitary definition of religion?

Until the late eighteenth century there was practically no attempt at defining religion *per se*. Consequently religions, particularly in the West, were defined by their cognitive content or dogmatic formulations. It is only with Friedrich Schleiermacher in the late eighteenth century that an attempt was made to define 'religion' as such by switching the emphasis from a cognitive or doctrinal emphasis to a more visceral or intuitive one. Schleiermacher defined religion as a 'feeling of absolute dependence'.[1] Since his day all attempts at a general definition of religion have relied heavily on emphasizing the intuitive, emotional or visceral.

73

A major step forward in the attempt at formulating a general definition of religion was the rise of anthropological and sociological theory. This approach asserted that religion is always embedded in a cultural matrix and that religious beliefs, customs, and rituals must be understood in a radical relationship to the cultures in which they arise. Durkheim in his *The Elementary Forms of the Religious Life* maintained that 'a society has all that is necessary to arouse the sensation of the divine in minds, merely by the power it has over them'.[2] Thus, in the Durkheimian analysis, religion is nothing more than a transform or expression of society. On the other hand psychologists from Freud to Skinner have seen in religion a projection either of various intrapsychic dynamics or of hopes and expectations based on previous experience.

From the turn of the twentieth century, however, scholars began to devote themselves to the phenomenology of religion on its own terms. They believed that there were phenomena that needed to be explained which eluded both sociological and psychological determinism. An example of such an approach has been to analyse religion in terms of an awareness of the 'sacred' and the 'holy'. Rudolf Otto, in his *The Idea of the Holy*, defined the essence of religious awareness as awe.[3] This he understood as a mixture of fear and fascination before the divine. Otto saw the essential religious experience as a *mysterium tremendum et fascinans*. However, Otto betrayed his Western origins by understanding this as a sensed 'wholly other' of the divine being. Such an approach began to get at a dominant form of Western mysticism, but was not so applicable to Eastern religions or to primitive ones. The most recent and subtle reworking of Otto's concept of the 'sacred' as the central core of all religious experience has been done by Mircea Eliade.[4] For Eliade, no longer is the sacred to be found almost exclusively in Otto's God-encounter type of experience. Rather, every culture exemplifies the existential sense of the sacred in its rituals and symbols, especially primitive and Asian cultures.

Commenting on Eliade, Winston King notes:

> It [the sacred] is embodied as sacred space, for example, in shrines and temples, in taboo areas, even limitedly in the erection of dwellings in accordance with a sense of the axis mundi, an orientation to the centre of the true 'sacred' universe. Indeed, structures often symbolically represent that physically invisible but most real of all universes – the

eternally perfect universe to which they seek to relate fruit-fully. This sense of sacredness often attaches to trees, stones, mountains, and other like objects in which mysterious power seems to reside. Many primitive rituals seek to sacramentally repeat the first moment of creation, often described in myth, when primordial chaos became recognizable order. Sacred time – that is, eternal and unfragmented time – is made vitally present by the reenactment of such myths. In *The Sacred and the Profane*, Eliade writes, 'every religious festival, every liturgical time, represents the reactualization of a sacred event that took place in a mythical past, in the beginning'.[5]

In fairness it must be stated that Eliade's position, though intriguing and subtle, is hard to verify in actual cases across cultures. Many anthropologists, linguists, and psychologists question whether the concept of the 'sacred' is identifiable as such in an analysis of the language, experience and thought of most primitive societies. Such scholars assert that religious experience is not *sui generis*, but is rather an amalgam of diverse cultural phenomena and experiences.

This cursory review of the history of our Western attempt to understand religion leaves us in a somewhat confused state. Perhaps the best current working definition of religion is given by Winston King in an attempt to define religious salvation. After first making the point that salvation is but another name for religion in general, he writes:

Are there distinguishing characteristics of religious salvation? The first is that religious salvation tends to concentrate on the needs that a culture defines as most fundamental, neglecting needs that a culture defines as less important. Religious means of salvation, often indirect and extrahuman, seek to use supersensible forces and powers either in addition to or in place of ordinary tangible means. The second distinguishing characteristic is that religious salvations tend to aim at total, absolute, and sometimes transcendent fulfillment of human needs. As defined by the cultural context, this fulfillment ranges all the way from the fullness of physical satisfactions to the eternal ecstasy of union with the Absolute.[6]

Neuropsychological Analysis of Religion

The above definition, derived as it is from the accumulated

insights of anthropologists, sociologists, psychologists, linguists, and phenomenologists, coincides with the conclusion from our work and that of others of our biogenetic structuralist colleagues that religious behaviour arises from the operation and interrelationship of two distinct neuroanatomical and neurophysiological mechanisms in the brain. The first of these is the perception of causal sequences in the organization of reality. This results in an attempt to impose control over the world through the manipulation of posited causal constructs such as gods, demons, spirits, or other personalized causal agencies.

The second mechanism is the result of neuropsychological evolution culminating in the potential to develop altered states of consciousness. Such experiences are often interpreted as glimpses into the world of the supernatural and tend to confirm the existence of the personalized power sources generated by the first (causal) mechanism just mentioned. Furthermore, in and of themselves, such experiences can often facilitate both a reorganization of the personality structure and a realignment of the individual towards the cosmos. We shall consider below both of these neuropsychological mechanisms and their interrelationship in the genesis of religions. First, however, we must examine what precisely a neuropsychological analysis of a 'universal' cultural institution such as religion is, and how it expands upon the usual anthropological, sociological, and ordinary psychological analysis of cultural institutions. A neuropsychological analysis, we hope, will not only give us a better understanding of the nature of religious experience and religious behaviour, but will also show us how cultural institutions other than religions, to a lesser or greater extent, can possess a 'religious' character.

In this chapter, we are proposing that there are two neuropsychological mechanisms which underlie the development of religious experiences and behaviours. These two classes of mechanisms represent two lines of neurological development involving the evolution of structures that comprise what we have called in other works the 'causal operator' on the one hand and the 'holistic operator' on the other. It is interesting that these two neural operators seem to generate the two essential characteristics in King's definition of religion, that is, the use of supersensible forces and powers to control the environment in such a way as to attain those needs which the culture defines as fundamental and, second, the tendency towards the fulfilment of human needs in a total, absolute, or transcendent fashion often involving unusual subjective states or experiences. We maintain that the first of these mechanisms, that is, the manipulation of the environment by manipulating the power of gods, spirits, or other personalized powers, is primarily aimed at self-maintenance. The second of these mechanisms is aimed primarily at self-transcendence, but also allows the temporary neurological destabilization requisite for the possibility of self-transformation. We will expand upon these in order.

Self-Maintenance: Control of the Environment through the Mediation of Personalized Power Sources

In previous papers, we have proposed the existence of a number of neural operators in the brain which are responsible for various higher cortical functions as well as the probable neuroanatomical substrate for these operators.[7] These operators include abstraction of generals from particulars, the perception of abstract causality in external reality, the perception of spatial or temporal sequences in external reality, and the ordering of elements of reality into causal chains giving rise to explanatory models of the external world whether scientific or mythical. Space does not permit us to recapitulate in detail the neurophysiological and neuroanatomical substrates of these operators.[8]

In essence the causal operator performs its functions on any given strip of reality in the same way that a mathematical operator functions. It organizes that strip of reality into what is subjectively perceived as causal sequences back to the initial terminus of that strip. In view of the apparently universal human trait, under ordinary circumstances, of positing causes for any given strip of reality, we postulate that if the initial terminus is not given by sense data, the causal operator generates automatically an initial terminus.

Western science differs only accidentally from the more usual form of human cognition. Science refuses to postulate an initial terminus or first cause for any strip of reality unless it is observed or can be immediately inferred from observation. Under more usual (non-scientific) conditions the causal operator generates the initial terminus or first cause of any strip of reality. That is, a mental construct drawn from elements encoded in memory and characterized by the nature of the operator itself. That is, the construct causes or in some sense has the power to generate the strip of reality. We are proposing that gods, powers, spirits, or, in general, what we have come to call personalized power sources, or any other causative construct are automatically generated by the causal operator. Note that in speaking of Western science we have not been speaking of Western scientists. The restrictions imposed on human thought in Western sciences are of a social and contractual nature. However, the brain of the scientist functions no differently from that of anyone else. Although he or she may reject the idea of gods, spirits, demons or any other type of personalized power source he or she nevertheless experiences them in dreams and fantasy life. Any practising psychiatrist or clinical psychologist can point to these phenomena in the fantasy life of the most rational person. The causal operator simply operates spontaneously on reality, positing an initial causal terminus when none is given. When the strip of reality to be analysed is the totality of the universe, then the initial terminus or first cause which is automatically produced by the causal operator is Aristotle's *First Mover Unmoved*.

If this analysis is essentially correct, then human beings have no choice but to construct myths peopled by personalized power sources to explain their world. The myths may be social in nature or they may be individual in terms of dreams, daydreams, or other fantasy aspects of the individual person. Nevertheless, as long as human beings are aware of the contingency of their existence in the face of what often appears to be a capricious universe, they must construct myths to orient themselves within that universe. Thus, they construct gods, spirits, demons, or other personalized power sources with whom they can deal contractually in order to gain control over a capricious environment. Once unknown or mysterious causes of strips of reality are perceived as persons or personalized forces, they can be dealt with as one would deal with powerful persons. They can be offered gifts in return for their beneficence. Thus, the concept of sacrifice in ancient Roman religion is the most primitive contractual obligation entered on by man with power sources or gods. All this is inherent in the obligatory functioning of the neurostructures we have just considered. Since it is unlikely that humankind will ever know the first cause of every strip of reality observed it is highly probable that it will always generate gods, powers, demons, or other entities as first causes to explain what it observes. Indeed, humans cannot do otherwise.

The development of higher cortical functions especially in the dominant hemisphere may be regarded as a blessing so far as they allow humans abstract problem solving, an adaptive mechanism in any environment. It can also be regarded as a curse. Because humans can think abstractly and causally they can transcend their immediate perceptual field. From experience, they can postulate probable events under given circumstances. Most of all, these functions make them acutely aware of their own mortality and of the contingency of their existence in an unpredictable world. This is the basis of the existential anxiety that humans bear within them. It is to relieve this 'curse of cognition', this existential anxiety, that humankind first seeks mastery over its environment by attempting to organize it mythically and by attempting to control it through the intervention of personalized power constructs. We can cite numerous examples from our own Judaeo-Christian tradition. In the early books of the Old Testament there are a number of references to Yahweh's being pleased by the 'sweet odour' or 'sweet fragrance' of the sacrifices offered to him. Indeed in some of the more primitive references the attention of Yahweh is sought by the fragrant odour of the sacrifice. Once his attention is obtained by the odour and by the gift, prayers may then be offered for whatever the original intention of the sacrifice may have been.

We maintain that this 'control' aspect of religion is a self-maintenance system. It may not be immediately obvious why this is so since clearly such attempts at controlling the world are probably not actually efficacious. At least they are not efficacious in producing the specific desired ends of those attempting to utilize the power of the god or gods. What is efficacious is the sense of control over the environment itself that such religious practices give. It is clear that the human psyche requires some sense of control over the environment in order not to become dispirited, discouraged, or even depressed. It has been noted by several researchers as well as by clinicians that the essence of a clinical depression is a sense of loss of control over one's life, over one's fate, or over the environment. We have presented the hypothesis in a previous work drawn from Sade's observations of his Macaque colony, that depression may have evolved in an attempt to give stability to primate groups. Thus, when an alpha male is challenged in an agonistic display, and when he loses the confrontation, he develops all the outward or behavioural signs of depression, complete with psychomotor retardation and movement to the periphery of the group. We have postulated that this state allows for the new alpha male to maintain his control over the group in a way that is unchallenged by the former holder of that position. This would seem to prevent prolonged and fierce power struggles which would disrupt the structure and function of the group. Whether this in fact is the origin of clinical depression among humans or not, it is certain that the sense of a loss of control of the environment is profoundly debilitating, paralysing and destructive.

We propose that the 'control' aspect of religion is the self-maintenance system *par excellence*, in that it allows for a sense of control over the environment which preserves the necessary positive psychological outlook to allow individuals and social groups to perform the actual manipulations in the external world which, in fact, do lead to some measure of control and ultimately to survival. This 'control' aspect of religion, involving the brain generating gods, spirits and powers and their manipulation via sacrifice, prayer and other contractual situations is probably the most primitive form of religion. It is the predominant form in primitive societies and during the early historic period, especially in the West. The example of early Roman religion is particularly pointed in that it was a state religion which concerned itself almost exclusively with the manipulation of Rome's deities for the purposes of the state. Although this control, manipulative, and contractual aspect of religion is very primitive and predominates in primitive societies and in the early historic phases of the higher cultures, it is nevertheless present, to some extent at least, even in the most developed and advanced religions. This is true both theoretically and certainly in terms of popular individual religious practice. We maintain that the attempt to control the environment via the positing of and control of personal power sources is sufficient in and of itself to constitute religion. In actual fact, almost all religions are comprised of other elements which we will address shortly. However, this aspect is never wholly absent, and, in and of itself, generates behaviours which can properly be called religious without any admixture of other elements. We are somewhat arbitrarily restricting the noun 'religion' and the adjective 'religious' to attempts to control the environment via personalized power sources.

We should note that the causal operator may also impose a spurious causality relating inanimate objects directly to each other, not through the mediation of personalized power sources. This process we have chosen to call magic and not religion. Thus, when a direct causal connection is seen between sticking a pin in a doll and a victim's having a heart attack we would call this magic. Religion, understood in the sense that we are presenting it, requires the mediation of the personalized power constructs. Thus, the *ex opere operantis* theory of sacramental efficacy of classic Protestantism – which focuses on the action of the person performing the rite – would be seen as a religious model whereas the *ex opere operato* theory of classic Roman Catholic sacramental theology – which focuses on the rite itself – would be seen as magical by this analysis.

Self-Transcendence: The Religious Interpretation of Altered States of Consciousness

There is a second neural mechanism which produces phenomena which are quite distinct from the 'control' aspect of religion but which are nevertheless seen as intrinsically religious when they occur. In fact, in all of the world's high religions the class of phenomena arising from this second neural mechanism is usually seen as expressing the summit or the ultimate in each respective religious tradition. In point of fact, however, it is extremely rare for this class of phenomena to exist independently from some aspect of religion generated by the 'control' mechanisms considered in the previous section. What we are alluding to here is what is often referred to as mystical phenomena or altered states of consciousness generating a sense of some interaction with another and mysterious world which in some way is perceived as ultimate or transcendent. Since the early 1960s there have been many attempts on the part of philosophers of religion and others to define mystical experiences and to categorize them. A fairly good general definition is given by Gimello (1978) as

> a mystical experience is a state of mind, achieved commonly through some sort of self-cultivation, of which the following are usually or often the salient, but not necessarily the only, features:

- A feeling of oneness or unity, variously defined.
- A strong confidence in the 'reality' or 'objectivity' of the experience, i.e. a conviction that it is somehow revelatory of 'the truth'.
- A sense of the final inapplicability to the experience of conventional language, i.e. a sense that the experience is ineffable.
- A cessation of normal intellectual operations (e.g. deduction, discrimination, ratiocination, speculation, etc.) or the substitution for them of some 'higher' or qualitatively different mode of intellect (e.g. intuition).
- A sense of the coincidence of opposites, of various kinds (paradoxically).

An extraordinarily strong affective tone, again of various kinds (e.g. sublime joy, utter serenity, great fear, incomparable pleasure, etc. – often an unusual combination of such as these).[9]

This will serve as a working definition of a mystical experience. Initially, many workers felt that mystical experiences are basically one and the same across cultures. Eventually, it became clear that there were various sorts of mystical experiences which seemed to be fundamentally different even allowing for the differences in cultural expression and the differences in interpretation of what happens during a mystical experience in terms of the religious tradition in which it is embedded. Thus, Frederick Streng in his *Language and Mystical Awareness* notes:

> The term mysticism has been used to refer to a variety of phenomena including occult experience, trance, a vague sense of unaccountable uneasiness, sudden extraordinary visions and words of divine beings, or aesthetic sensitivity. For our purposes, we will narrow the definition to: an interior illumination of reality that results in ultimate freedom. Ninian Smart has correctly distinguished mysticism in this sense from 'the experience of a dynamic external presence'.[10]

We would like to pick up on this commentary regarding Smart's distinction between the experience of Otto's 'wholly other' and the internal sense of ineffable unity defined as a mystical experience, predominantly although not exclusively, in oriental traditions. Smart[11] has argued that certain strains of Hinduism, Buddhism and Taoism differ markedly from prophetic religions such as Judaism and Islam and from religions related to the prophetic-like Christianity, in that the religious experience most characteristic of the former is 'mystical' whereas that most characteristic of the latter is 'numinous'. Of these two terms, it is the numinous which Smart seems to have an easier time explaining, since it obviously arises more spontaneously out of Western religious traditions.

Somewhat similar to Smart's distinction between the mystical experience, properly so called, and the numinous experience is that of W. B. Stace,[12] who distinguishes between what he calls extrovertive mystical experiences and introvertive mystical experiences. Stace characterizes these respectively as follows:

Extrovertive mystical experiences:

1 The Unifying Vision – things are one
2 The more concrete apprehension of the One as an inner subjectivity, or life, in all things
3 Sense of objectivity or reality
4 Blessedness, peace, etc.
5 Feeling of the holy, sacred, or divine
6 Paradoxicality
7 Alleged by mystics to be ineffable.

Introvertive mystical experiences:

1 The Unitary Consciousness; the One, the Void; pure consciousness
2 Nonspatial, nontemporal
3 Sense of objectivity or reality
4 Blessedness, peace, etc.
5 Feeling of the holy, sacred, or divine
6 Paradoxicality
7 Alleged by mystics to be ineffable.

Stace then concludes that characteristics 3 to 7 are identical in the two lists and are therefore universal common characteristics of mysticism in all cultures, ages, religions, and civilizations of the world. However, it is in characteristics 1 and 2 that the distinction is made between extrovertive mystical experiences and introvertive mystical experiences in his typology. One can easily see a similarity between Stace's extrovertive mystical experience and Smart's numinous experience and between Stace's introvertive mystical experiences and Smart's mystical experience proper.

In Steven Katz's critique of both Smart's and Stace's typology[13] he asserts that not only are those critics naïve who maintain that all mystical experiences are essentially one, but that even Smart's and Stace's typology do not do justice to the variety and essential differences of mystical experiences as presented in the literature. Katz maintains that not only do mystical experiences differ in terms of the language of the culture in which they are embedded in explaining them, but their very content is altered by the cultural experience the mystic brings to them.

All of this presents a rather confused picture about what, if anything, mystical experiences may have in common across cultures. We feel that a neuropsychological analysis of mysticism and altered states of consciousness in general can bring some order out of the confusion by attempting to set up a typology of mystical experiences based on the underlying brain functions which seem to generate such experiences.

In a number of works[14] we, along with other colleagues, have proposed that rhythmicity in the environment, be it visual, auditory, tactile, or proprioceptive drives the sympathetic–ergotropic system to maximal capacity with intermittent spillover and simultaneous activation of the parasympathetic-trophotropic system creating unusual subjective states. For the most part, here, we are discussing ceremonial ritual. One of the things that happens is progressive activation of certain parts of the non-dominant parieto-occipital region of the brain (which we have called the 'holistic operator')[15] creating an increasing sense of wholeness progressively more and more dominant over the sense of multiplicity of baseline reality. Because of alterations in prefrontal cortical functioning, the baseline sense of ordinary time can be altered in a number of ways. We have discussed the complex effects of rhythmicity and entrainment of brain waves elsewhere.[16] Several points, however, ought to be noted here.

Activation of the holistic operator and the attainment of certain ecstatic and blissful states can be strongly reinforced, if not totally achieved, via other mechanisms. Thus, meditation approaches the situation from the direction opposite from ceremonial ritual and highly rhythmic behaviour. Meditation drives the parasympathetic–trophotropic system to saturation and spillover with simultaneous activation of the sympathetic–ergotropic system. In any case, the end result can be the same in both the ritual and meditative situations.[17] Likewise, the use of incense and other powerful fragrances directly affects the limbic system which, in fact, in the old neurological terminology used to be called the rhinencephalon or the nose brain. There are a number of connections both direct and indirect between the olfactory bulb and various mid-brain-limbic structures including the median forebrain bundle. This latter structure is generally considered a major 'pleasure centre', and it has been shown that rats would much rather stimulate it than eat. In fact, rats can die of starvation by overstimulating their median forebrain bundles and not taking enough time out for nourishment. The stimulation of the olfactory bulbs and adjacent structures by the use of incense represents a powerful synergistic mechanism to both rhythmicity and meditation in the production of ecstatic unitary states.

And *unitary states* is the name of the game. The bottom line in understanding the phenomenology of subjective religious experience is to understand that every religious experience involves a sense of the unity of reality at least somewhat greater than the baseline perception of unity in day to day life.[18] This is another way of saying that a more intense application of the holistic operator to incoming stimuli, over and above its baseline function, coupled with the limbic or emotional stimulation that accompanies such increased functioning, always results in experiences which are described as religious or spiritual in varying degrees. Whatever the mechanism for the increased functioning of the holistic operator may be, whether it is rhythmicity and entrainment of brain waves, profound meditation, olfactory stimulation in certain contexts, extreme fasting or electrolyte imbalance, the bottom line is stimulation of the holistic operator with accompanying experiences of increased unity over multiplicity.

A previous paper[19] describes eight primary epistemic or knowing states, and particularly contrasted our baseline epistemic state with the rare mystical state which we call Absolute Unitary Being (AUB). AUB is a state described in the mystical literature of all the world's great religions. When a person is in that state he or she loses all sense of discrete being and even the difference between self and other is obliterated. There is no sense of the passing of time, and all that remains is a perfect timeless undifferentiated consciousness. When such a state is suffused with positive affect there is a tendency to describe the experience, after the fact, as personal. Hence, such experiences are often described as a perfect union with God (the *Unio mystica* of the Christian tradition) or else the perfect manifestation of God in the Hindu tradition. When such experiences are accompanied by neutral affect they tend to be described, after the fact, as impersonal, generating concepts such as the abyss of Jacob Boeme, the Void or Nirvana of Buddhism or the Absolute of a number of philosophical and mystical traditions. There is no question that whether the experience is interpreted personally as God or impersonally as the Absolute it nevertheless possesses a quality of transcendent wholeness without any temporal or spatial division whatsoever.

We have postulated that these rare states of AUB are attained through the 'absolute' functioning of the holistic operator.[20]

In absolute Unitary Being, not only would there be maximum discharge from the holistic operator generating a sense of absolute wholeness, but there would be an intense firing of structures associating with that wholeness the intense consciousness of the reflexive ego. Thus, the experience of Absolute Unitary Being is not a vague sense of undifferentiated wholeness but one of intense consciousness, since both systems are maximally firing. If this model is correct, it should be obvious that AUB involves an extreme state of functioning of the holistic operator. More usual or ordinary perceptions reflect some sort of balance between analytic and synthetic or gestalt perception.

We propose, however, that even in more normal perceptions, whenever the sense of wholeness exceeds the sense of multiplicity of parts or of discrete elements in the sensorium, there is an affective discharge via the right brain-limbic connections that Schwartz et al.[21] have shown to be of such importance. This tilting of the balance towards an increased perception of wholeness, depending on its intensity, can be experienced as beauty, romantic love, numinosity or the religious awe described by Smart, religious exaltation in the perception of unity in multiplicity (described by Stace as extrovertive mystical experience), all merging into various trance states. We are proposing that there is an aesthetic–religious spectrum, and that the point on this spectrum that any perception has depends on how far tilted it is in the direction of wholeness.[22] In other words, the more the holistic operator functions in excess of a state of balance with the analytic functions of the left hemisphere the stronger will be the associated emotional charge. Thus, in any aesthetic perception, whether it is a piece of music, a painting, a sculpture, or the perception of a sunset, there is a sense of meaning and wholeness which transcends the constituent parts. In aesthetic perceptions, however, this transcendence is slight to moderate. We would locate the overarching sense of unity between two persons in romantic love as the subsequent stage in this aesthetic–religious continuum. In the next stage, the holistic operator functions with a degree of intensity which generates a very marked sense of meaning and wholeness extending well beyond the parts perceived or well beyond the image generated but in a 'wholly other' context.

This experience Jung characterized as numinosity or religious awe. Both Otto and Smart have described this experience in detail. It is often considered (rather incorrectly we feel) to be the dominant Western mystical experience. It is experienced when an archetypal symbol is perceived or when certain archetypal elements are externally constellated in a myth. It is an experience during which the connotation of what is perceived vastly exceeds the denotation. As we move from numinosity along the spectrum, that is, as the function of the holistic operator more and more overwhelms synthetic perception, we reach the state of religious exaltation which Bucke has called Cosmic Consciousness. This state is characterized by a sense of meaning and wholeness extending to all discrete being whether subjective or objective. The essential unity and purposefulness of the universe is perceived as a primary datum in spite of knowledge of, and the perception of, evil in the world. During this state there is nothing whatsoever that escapes the mantle of wholeness and purposefulness. But this state does not obliterate discrete being, and it certainly exists within a temporal matrix. This roughly corresponds to Stace's extrovertive mystical experience.

As we move beyond the state of religious exaltation and cosmic consciousness, we move into the realm of trance states where the increased sense of unity begins to obliterate the boundaries between perceived entities both in the external environment and especially the boundaries between self and other. Examples of such trance states include the states achieved by members of flagellant sects during the Middle Ages, by the states known to be achieved by Taiwanese mediums, and by states attained by practitioners of Voodoo in Haiti and the Umbanda of Brazil. Certainly, trance states can exist in varying degrees involving a mild blurring of boundaries at one end all the way to merging into the state of absolute unitary being at the other. Absolute Unitary Being represents the extreme of the aesthetic–religious continuum and the absolute functioning of the holistic operator. During this final state there is nothing but a timeless and perfect sense of meaning and wholeness without any perception of discrete entities. One might call AUB the ultimate trance. It is the mystical experience properly so-called of Ninian Smart and the introvertive mystical experience of W. T. Stace.

It is clear that all these experiences in one way or another involve self-transcendence. This is the second manifestation of religious systems. Theoretically, it can stand on its own but rarely if ever does. It is usually integrated in one form or another, at least minimally, with the first aspect of religion mentioned above, that is attempt at control of the external environment. One might ask why one would wish to transcend oneself. It is intuitively obvious why human beings would wish to control their environment. It is not immediately so obvious why one would wish to transcend the self. The answer, however, is obvious to those who have had mystical experiences. It is clear that such experiences are characterized, at the lower end of the aesthetic–religious spectrum, by a sense of insight into the world of the mysterious bordering on the supernatural, and at the extreme end of the spectrum by a sense of attaining absolute reality, union with God or the Absolute, a sense of either bliss or utter tranquillity, and, perhaps most important of all, a lack of fear of death. It is almost universally reported from those who have experienced the final two stages of the aesthetic–religious spectrum, that is, either cosmic consciousness or absolute unitary being, that they simply have no fear of death. This is not necessarily because they believe in an afterlife. They may or they may not believe in an afterlife, depending on the general structure of the religious belief which they hold separate from their mystical experiences. Even if they do not believe in a specific afterlife, mystical experiences tend to generate a sense of the ultimate goodness and appropriateness of reality, and death is simply perceived as an ordinary part of that reality, something which is not feared. Thus, it is easy to see why self-transcendence is highly prized. To a greater or lesser extent it makes an individual invulnerable to the exigencies of life and to the effects of evil in the world.

It is something of a paradox that this second manifestation of religion, at least toward the end of the aesthetic–religious spectrum, seems to involve a surrender to God, the Absolute, or to the universal fact of ultimate reality. It is in some ways the opposite of the first manifestation of religion that we considered in this chapter, that is, the attempt to control the environment. Paradoxically, it represents a surrender to absolute reality. In its more perfect or complete forms, this second aspect of religion positively rejects any attempt at control of the physical universe or even of one's own life as being inimical to spiritual development. This being the case, it is curious that rarely does either the first or second manifestation of religion stand on its own. In real cultures they are integrated to a greater or lesser extent. The first manifestation of religion, control of the environment, is more likely to stand on its own, but even in primitive religions shamans or witch-doctors enter into the 'other world' of the gods and spirits and return to testify to its reality. Indeed, it is not too difficult to see how the second or mystical manifestation of religion can help the first. In so far as altered states of consciousness can be perceived as experiencing the world of the gods, they can be seen as immediate empirical verification of the existence of the personal power sources which are automatically constructed by the causal operator. It is not so immediately obvious why those religions which are primarily mystical in nature tolerate a significant admixture of the first or 'control' manifestation of religion. The answer is probably that human beings are human beings. Religions are not primarily composed of mystics or people who have attained advanced spiritual states. They are composed by and large of ordinary people who must face ordinary problems in life. For them the control of the environment represents a necessity of day-to-day living. They may occasionally experience altered states at the lower end of the aesthetic–religious continuum. These experiences may add credence to the powerful witness of mystics. But for the ordinary person such experiences, and the testimony of mystics, function to support the power of the gods or personalized power sources. It is, thus, that mystical religion tends to reinforce the first manifestation of religion, that is, the control of the environment.

Self-Transformation: A Fundamental Change of Understanding

Self-transformation is not so much a third manifestation of religious systems as it is a consequence and corollary of self-transcendence. As individuals move up the aesthetic–religious continuum and impose ever more holistic views on reality, there is noted an increased emotional discharge via the rich connections which Schwartz et al.[23] have described between the non-dominant hemisphere and the limbic system. This increased emotional discharge, excitement if you will, is known to cause a certain degree of neural instability allowing for the forming of new dendratic neuronal connections, even resulting in a realignment of one's understanding of one's self to the world. In other words, a state of relatively sustained emotional excitement can facilitate the reorganization of our cognized environment. This is akin to what Anthony Wallace called Mazeway Resynthesis and to what the great psychoanalyst Franz Alexander called a corrective emotional experience.

Any intense emotional arousal such as the 'hitting bottom' of Alcoholics Anonymous can facilitate a personal transformation. Such an experience, however, is accompanied by a surrender of the ego in one way or another to a higher power. This may be to the general process in psychoanalysis, to the higher power in Alcoholics Anonymous, or to a more traditional concept of God. But there is no doubt that heightened emotionality in a context of surrender increases the possibility of self-transformation. One does not have to move far up the aesthetic–religious continuum for the possibility of transformation to become more and more probable. Indeed at the extremes of the aesthetic–religious continuum, transformation of one's life becomes almost inevitable. We know of no mystics, properly so called, who attained the levels of either cosmic consciousness or absolute unitary being, whose views of themselves and the world were not radically transformed. But even more ordinary religious experiences, including extremely intense aesthetic experiences, can often catalyse self-transformation to more desirable alignments of the self to the cosmos.

Other Activities Perceived as Religious

Other activities may be perceived as more or less religious, or having a religious flavour, in so far as they utilize the same neurological mechanisms which are manifested most strongly in either the first or second aspects of religious systems described above. That is, as a human activity exerts control over the physical environment or in so far as it involves the union of the self with other persons or things, such an activity can be perceived as having a religious flavour or even as being strongly although not essentially religious. Sports, politics, science, or almost any human activity which utilizes the mechanisms of either control of the environment or of imposing relative unity over multiplicity can be considered religious under certain circumstances. Furthermore, any activity, whether or not it involves control of the physical environment or the theme of unity, can be perceived as religious if it is perceived as contributing to humanity's fundamental sense of well being. This is because religion either in its first or second manifestation is paradigmatic in this regard. Indeed as King pointed out in his definition of religion, all religion tends to fulfil the fundamental needs of an individual as defined by the culture often in an absolute or transcendent way. Since this fundamental need-fulfilment role is essential to religion, any activity which participates in satisfying fundamental needs can be seen as participating in the religious paradigm.

Conclusion

We hope that this chapter can help provide an understanding of how a neuropsychological analysis of what Murdock calls a 'universal cultural institution' (in this case religion) can be helpful in clearing up confusion which is often generated by a purely phenomenological analysis. An understanding of the brain mechanisms underlying various aspects of cultural phenomena seems to have a more powerful explanatory force than factor analysis or other methodological approaches at a phenomenological level. Our neuropsychological analysis has focused on the two essential manifestations of religious systems, that is, the imposition of control over the external world and the drive for an increased perception of unity over diversity in altered subjective states.

PART TWO

Broader
Reflections

Chapter Seven

SCIENCE AND RELIGION: CONTEST OR CONFIRMATION?

John Bowker

The relationship between science and religion has been described in various ways, falling between two extremes. At one extreme, the relationship is seen as one of warfare, as in the titles of two nineteenth-century books, J. W. Draper's *History of the Conflict Between Religion and Science* (1874), and A. D. White's *A History of the Warfare of Science With Theology* (1896). At this extreme, science is understood to have engaged religion in a series of encounters, usually taken to begin with Galileo, but often taken still further back to Lucretius or to the Greek atomists. In any case, the warfare model sees a progressive campaign (and often the words 'progressive' and 'progress' are freely used) in which science drives back the frontiers of ignorance and superstition. It is Edward Lear's campaign against 'the screamy ganders of the church, who put darkness forward and insist that it is light'.[1] The physicist, Robert Stoneley, writing in Naomi Mitchison's review of all knowledge, entitled *Outline for Boys and Girls and Their Parents*, said of religions that they came into being because people used to reason falsely. He then continued:

> Now, we might write all sorts of beautiful stories about how the world began, something like the Indian story that the earth is carried on the back of an elephant, which stumbles every now and then, and so causes earthquakes. The trouble would be that, as more and more facts were found out, it would get harder and harder to write the stories, for they would begin to contradict one another. On the other hand, the scientist . . .[2]

At the other extreme are those who take the view that since there is only one common subject-matter, namely the cosmos and human life within it, religions are necessarily early and somewhat more intuitive accounts of that some subject-matter. While science may therefore correct the inevitable mistakes of the earlier accounts, in essentials science confirms the basic intuitions of religion. So we find Amaury de Riencourt writing in *The Eye of Shiva: Eastern Mysticism and Science*:

> The new picture of the universe disclosed by contemporary physics appears to be largely in accord with Eastern metaphysics. . . . It might well be that mankind is now on the threshold of a psychological and physiological revolution of a magnitude that will overshadow all the social and political revolutions of our century – made possible by the seemingly incongruous, yet perfectly logical marriage between science and Eastern mysticism's insights.[3]

These two extremes, however, are not so far apart as they may, at first sight, seem. Both of them give priority to science as the paradigmatic way of establishing true knowledge. In the second extreme, this is more concealed, but it is there, nevertheless, because what is being claimed in effect is that religions are validated by the extent to which they are in accord with modern science – in this case, physics and cosmology. It is this understanding of the relationship between science and religion which gives rise to attempts at reconciliation and translation. In some, the concepts of science are given the role of God, so that science becomes 'a new religion' (see Mary Hesse, Chapter 8). In others, religions are understood as well-winnowed systems of human wisdom (wisdom often being understood as that which has delivered scientific achievement, or more broadly, as that which has conferred advantage in the process of evolution under the control of natural selection); if that religious wisdom is to continue in the post-Newtonian and post-Darwinian world, it must be translated into the concepts of science, abandoning that which is incompatible with the scientific world-view. An example of this is the work of Ralph Burhoe and of the Institute on Religion in an Age of Science. In the first editorial of the Institute's journal, *Zygon*, Burhoe wrote:

> We respond to the growing fears that the widening chasm in twentieth-century culture between values and knowledge, or good and truth, or religion and science, is disruptive if not

lethal for human destiny. In this split, the traditional faiths and philosophies, which once informed people of what is of most sacred concern for them, have lost their credibility and hence their power. Yet human fulfilment or salvation in the age of science requires not less but more insight and conviction concerning life's basic values and moral requirements.

These ways of describing the relationship between science and religion are so common that there is no need to exemplify them any further. What is obvious is that they do not exhaust *all* the possibilities. There are many other ways in which science and religion might be related. There might, for example, be *no* relationship: they may be so different as human enterprises that they are simply incommensurable. Or again, there may be no such 'thing' as science and no such 'thing' as religion to be related. Both science and religion cover widely different enterprises. The different theories and activities that might be described as scientific may, each in their own way, have different ways of being related to the different theories and activities that might be described as religious. There will not be one way, and one way only, in which something called 'science' and something called 'religion' are related. Lucretius did indeed attack religion – that is, what he called *religio*:

> *Tantum religio potuit suadere malorum . . .*
> *Religio peperit scelerosa atque impia facta*[4]

But what Lucretius had in mind was the sacrifice of Iphigenia at Aulis as a demonstration of the disastrous consequences of an over-scrupulous insistence on the exact detail of ritual. There is no fixed meaning of religion (see the opening remarks in my Introduction to *The Oxford Dictionary of World Religions*, Oxford University Press, 1997, p. xv), nor for that matter of science, which makes them available for comparison through the ages.

Inevitably, therefore, we are dealing with human constructions: what *do* we describe as scientific? What *do* we describe as religious? These questions are not to be dismissed as a quaint pedantry of definition. What we have in mind as science and what we have in mind as religion will clearly affect how we think they can be related. If, for example, we believe that both are systems for the development of empirical propositions about putative matters of fact concerning the same subject-matter, namely, human nature and the cosmos, then obviously we will end up with a warfare model of the relationship. If we confine science to physics, cosmology, evolution and genetics, then we will clearly have a very narrow conversation with religion, especially if religion is identified with Christianity. If we suppose that science alone has a legitimate claim to truth, and that consequently it alone has authority to say what the world is and how human lives within it should be lived, then we are close to making science into a new religion – as Samuel Butler perceived:

> Science is being daily more and more personified and anthropomorphised into a god. By and by they will say that science took our nature upon him, and sent down his only begotten son, Charles Darwin, or Huxley, into the world so that those who believe in him, etc.; and they will burn people for saying that science, after all, is only an expression for our ignorance of our own ignorance.[5]

We begin to see that there is a great deal more to be addressed theoretically in the study of science and religion than we have so far uncovered in any of the simplified styles that are prevalent now. What science and religion are *about* is a fundamental question. It is, however, a question that cannot be answered unless we appreciate the extent to which, in the debate between science and religion, we inherit our agendas from the past – and the extent, also, to which those inherited agendas then dominate the nature and content of the debate.

The purpose, therefore, of this chapter is to look at the way in which our own agenda has been set for us. This means attending, first, to the way in which the great schism opened up in the nineteenth century between science on the one side, and myth, poetry and music on the other, since this has set so much of the agenda for our own perception of the relation between science and religion. It will show us, on the way, why some people in 1914 would eat nothing for some hours before going to see a performance of Wagner's *Parsifal*. At the end, I intend to suggest, with an example, what might happen if we refuse that agenda, and if instead we attempt to look at the relationship in a different way.

Let us begin, then, by going back to the nineteenth century and standing on the top of Mount Sinai, in the company of Arthur Clough. Clough is the nineteenth-century poet of the revised ten commandments, 'The Latest Decalogue':

Thou shalt have one God only; who
Would be at the expense of two? ...
Thou shalt not kill; but needst not strive
Officiously to keep alive ...

and of this poem, 'When Israel came out of Egypt':

And as of old from Sinai's top
   God said that God is One,
By Science strict so speaks He now
   To tell us, There is None!
Earth goes by chemic forces; Heaven's
   A Mécanique Céleste!
And heart and mind of human kind
   A watch-work as the rest!

Clough's reference to *la mécanique céleste* is, of course, to the famous work of that title by Laplace. In it he had dismissed the worry of Newton that perturbations in the planetary orbits would lead to instability in the solar system; and with the worry he had also evidently dismissed God, since divine intervention was no longer needed to ensure stability – hence his familiar reply to Napoleon's complaint that he had left God out of his system, 'Sire, I have no need of that hypothesis.' In a mechanistic universe, in which theoretically one might have a complete knowledge of the state of the universe and of the laws of nature, every detail of the future becomes predictable; and in that case, even if God existed, he would not be able to intervene in any way. If that mechanistic philosophy is applied to human nature (as Lemaitre did apply it, in the inevitably entitled work, *L'homme machine*), then we arrive at Clough's further reference, 'the heart and mind of human kind a watch-work as the rest'.

It was this mechanistic philosophy, combined with its application in the successive miracles of technology, which gave rise to the great vision that science had become the only valid purveyor of true propositions about the universe, and that it would extend its accounts of truth to all aspects of the universe, including human life and history within it. What is called 'the nomothetic ambition' became in the nineteenth century pervasive – the ambition to discern and apply *nomoi*, laws, as invariant as the Newtonian law of gravity to all phenomena. It seems bizarre now, but that is what Freud set out to become, the Newton of the inside of the human head.[6]

It is this vision also which produced what is sometimes

known as 'scientism', a word now somewhat in disgrace, but roughly the view that science alone produces true and valid knowledge, and that other claims to knowledge must be tested for truth against science – a view well caught in John Tyndall's address to the British Association in 1874:

> The impregnable position of science may be described in a few words. We claim, and we shall wrest from theology, the entire domain of cosmological theory. All schemes and systems which thus infringe upon the domain of science must, in so far as they do this, submit to its control, and relinquish all thought of controlling it.[7]

But since science at the time was inclined to answer the question, 'What is the scope of science?', with the same single word with which Quine was later to answer the question of ontology, 'What is there?' – namely, 'Everything' – not much scope was left to theology.

Of course God could be rescued as the great designer, who both designs the boat, and then, as a dignitary in a large hat, also launches it. But after that he can do nothing but bid it farewell and allow it to sail away across the oceans of time, obedient to the impervious laws of motion. Something like that is what is known as 'deism'. Deism does indeed rescue God from complete oblivion. But it is an understanding of God far removed from the love affair between the human and the divine which George Herbert envisaged, 'Love bade me welcome; yet my soul drew back . . .'. For that reason, Herman Melville wrote to Hawthorne in 1851: 'The reason the mass of men fear God, and at bottom dislike Him, is because they rather distrust His heart, and fancy Him all brain, like a watch.' He then added in parenthesis: '(You perceive I employ a capital initial in the pronoun referring to the Deity: don't you think there is a slight dash of flunkeyism in that usage?)'[8]

A God with a brain like a watch is not, as Whitehead once observed of Aristotle's God, very available for worship, let alone for love. But in a Newtonian universe, it seemed obvious that while the God of Deism may wind up the universe and set it in motion, he cannot interfere in its process. An Act of God can only be (as A. P. Herbert defined it in *Uncommon Law*) 'something which no reasonable man could have expected'. What reasonable people of the nineteenth century *could* expect to see, and *did* see, was a spectacular consequence of Newtonian science in technology, miracles achieved more by human enterprise than by divine intervention. In that same year, 1851, the Great Exhibition was held in London to illustrate and to celebrate those achievements. The Catalogue to the Exhibition quoted at the beginning the speech of Prince Albert which had set the whole project in motion:

> So man is approaching a more complete fulfilment of that great and sacred mission which he has to perform in this world. His reason being created after the image of God, he has to use it to discover the laws by which the Almighty governs His creation, and, by making those laws his standard of action, to conquer Nature to his use – himself a divine instrument. Science discovers these laws of power, motion, and transformation; industry applies them to the raw matter, which the earth yields us in abundance, but which becomes valuable only by knowledge: art teaches us the immutable laws of beauty and symmetry, and gives to our productions forms in accordance with them.

But why the continuing genuflections in the direction of God? Why the flunkeyism? No doubt the occasion of Prince Albert's speech was a ritual occasion, a speech in the Guildhall. But what the theological claim comes down to is a claim that God created humans who created the Great Exhibition. Why not simply say that humans created the Great Exhibition? In which case, why not see this as a better manifestation of the Kingdom of God than anything achieved in the ages of faith?

That, or something very close to it, was the conclusion reached by Charles Kingsley, who, when he visited the Great Exhibition, was moved to tears. To him, he said later, 'It was like going into a sacred place.' Four days later, he preached a sermon in which he said:

> If these forefathers of ours could rise from their graves this day, they would be inclined to see in our hospitals, in our railroads, in the achievements of our physical science, confirmation of that old superstition of theirs, proofs of the kingdom of God, realisations of the gifts which Christ received for men, vaster than any of which they had dreamed.[9]

In that same year, his novel *Yeast* had appeared, which contains the letter written by Lancelot Smith to a Roman Catholic, which makes the contrast equally explicit:

When your party compare sneeringly Romish Sanctity and English Civilisation, I say, 'Take your Sanctity, and give me the Civilisation! . . . Give me the political economist, the sanitary reformer, the engineer; and take your saints and virgins, relics and miracles. The spinning jenny and the railroad, Cunard's liners and the electric telegraph, are to me, if not to you, signs that we are, on some points at least, in harmony with the universe; that there is a mighty spirit working among us, who cannot be your anarchic and destroying Devil, and therefore may be the Ordering and Creating God.[10]

'May be'. But it may also be an entirely human enterprise, without need of God, and often, in practice, achieved without reference to God at all. When Brindley had a problem with the engineering of his great canals, he would, according to John Aiken, 'retire to his bed, where in perfect solitude he would lie for one, two, or three days, pondering the matter in his mind, till the requisite expedient had presented itself'.[11] There is no evidence that he devoted much, or indeed any, of that time to prayer.

It is this exile of God from effect, from being causative in this world unless, may be, through the enterprise of human skill – this relegation of God to what Leslie Stephen called 'a mere *roi fainéant*, a constitutional king, secured from our sight by responsible ministers in the shape of second causes' – which led Matthew Arnold to talk, in a famous phrase, of the failure of the religious fact:

There is not a creed which is not shaken, not an accredited dogma which is not shown to be questionable, not a received tradition which does not threaten to dissolve. Our religion has materialised itself in the supposed fact; it has attached its emotion to the fact, and now the fact is failing it.[12]

In a literally dis-spiriting sentence (itself an early instance of a translation programme), he observed that 'for science, God is simply *the stream of tendency by which all things seek to fulfil the law of their being*'.[13]

What facts had failed? Winwoode Reade answered that question in his book, *The Martyrdom of Man*, which appeared in 1872. It is a history of the world, written under the influence of Darwin, in which he made this summary:

As time passed on, the belief of the first Christians that the end of the world was near at hand became fainter and gradually died away. It was then declared that God had favoured the earth with a respite of one thousand years. In the meantime the gospel or good tidings which the Christians announced was this. There was one God, the Creator of the world. He had long been angry with men because they were what he had made them. But he sent his only begotten son into a corner of Syria, and because his son had been murdered his wrath had been partly appeased. He would not torture to eternity all the souls that he had made; he would spare at least one in every million that were born. Peace unto earth and goodwill unto men if they would act in a certain manner; if not, fire and brimstone and the noisome pit ... This creed with the early Christians was not a matter of half-belief and metaphysical debate, as it is at the present day, when Catholics and Protestants discuss hell-fire with courtesy and comfort over filberts and port wine. To those credulous and imaginative minds God was a live king, hell a place in which real bodies were burnt with real flames, which was filled with the sickening stench of roasted flesh, which resounded with agonising shrieks. They saw their fathers and mothers, their sisters and their dearest friends, hurrying onward to that fearful pit unconscious of danger, laughing and singing, lured on by the fiends whom they called the gods. . . . The Christians of that period felt more and did more than those of the present day, not because they were better men but because they believed more; and they believed more because they knew less. Doubt is the offspring of knowledge: 'the savage never doubts at all.'

Reade had no doubt how great the pain and anguish will be as the facts fail. His book concludes:

A season of mental anguish is at hand, and through this we must pass in order that our posterity may rise. The soul must be sacrificed; the hope in immortality must die. A sweet and charming illusion must be taken from the human race, as youth and beauty vanish never to return.

The young Winston Churchill protested, 'Reade was right, but wrong to say it! The human race must be allowed to keep its illusions.' Freud, reflecting a little later on what he took to be 'the future of an illusion', did not think so: we must be educated into reality. Others allowed doubt to deconstruct dogma, but could not quite let go. In that same year, 1872, Tennyson spoke to two friends of what he was prepared to call 'that beautiful illusion' of immortality: 'If I ceased to believe in any chance of another life, and of a great Personality somewhere in the universe, I should not care for anything.' Even Kingsley drew back from the brink, saying that if God turned out to be a deceiver, 'I'd go and blow my brains out and be rid of the whole thing at once, I would indeed.'

A few did exactly that. Winwoode Reade also wrote a novel, just before his death in 1875, called *The Outcast*, and this, being based on his own experience, gives a vivid illustration of this desolation of a once familiar world:

> Arthur Elliott was the only son of a wealthy landed proprietor, one of my nearest neighbours, and a brother magistrate. Arthur had a most amiable nature, and was tenderly loved, not only by his parents, but by all who knew him intimately. His attainments were remarkable, as I can testify; for we read much together. He was an excellent classical scholar, but his favourite study was that of metaphysics, from which he was led to the study of natural science. But religion was the poetry and passion of his life; and though of a different belief, it afforded me pleasure to hear him discourse on the grandeur and benevolence of God. Sometimes when we were together in a deep green wood on a sultry summer afternoon; or sometimes walking at night beneath the glorious starlit sky; or sometimes, when reading the dialogues of Plato, some divine thought rose from the book like an immortal spirit from the grave, and passed into the soul, then the tears would stream from his eyes, and falling on his knees he would utter praises or prayers in words of surpassing eloquence, and with a voice of sweetest melody. And often – how well I remember it now – often at such time his gestures grew wild and almost furious, his utterance was choked, and a strange bubbling sound came from his mouth . . .

> One day he came to me in trouble. He had been reading the great work of Malthus – the *Essay on Population* – and said that it made him doubt the goodness of God. I replied with the usual commonplace remarks; he listened to me attentively, then shook his head, and went away. A little while afterwards he read *The Origin of Species*, which had just come out, and

which proves that the law of population is the chief agent by which evolution has been produced. From that time he began to show symptoms of insanity – which disease it is thought he inherited from one of his progenitors. He dressed always in black, and said that he was in mourning for mankind. The works of Malthus and Darwin, bound in sombre covers, were placed on a table in his room; the first was lettered outside, *The Book of Doubt*, and the second *The Book of Despair* . . .

In the grey hour of dawn they heard a struggle in the room, and a choked kind of cry. They pushed the door, but it had been secured from within by a small piece of wood wedged in underneath. They forced it open at last, and the body of the unfortunate young man was found hanging from the window bar. Life was extinct.

The Book of Doubt, The Book of Despair. What seemed increasingly obvious, and not only to Reade, was that a third book could no longer be placed on the table, this one bound in bright covers, the Bible, lettered on the outside, the Book of Hope. For the traditional claims for the Bible, that it is inerrant, literally true and verbally inspired, had come to seem as obviously spurious as the claim of the Qur'an to be the same. Indeed, Carlyle argued that the Qur'an had a better claim to those descriptions, since Muslims do at least live according to its words, whereas few Christians (at least in Carlyle's opinion) exemplify the Gospels in the way they live.

More seriously, in 1835, there appeared D. F. Strauss's *Life of Jesus Critically Examined*, the book which, it has been said, produced for him both fame and ruin: he became well-known enough to be appointed to a Chair at Zurich, and far too notorious to be able to take up the appointment. In 1835 also, the first railway was opened in Germany, running twenty kilometres between Fürth and Nürnberg. Strauss saw the two events, the book and the railway, as being connected. Writing to a friend about his own first journey on the line, he wrote:

Five hours in half-an-hour. Impressive significance of the modern miracle, dreamy consciousness during the modern flight. No fear but a feeling of inner kinship between my own principles and that of the discovery.[14]

Strauss accepted that the science which produces steam and engines has the right to determine truth. In the Preface to his *Life of Jesus*, he wrote:

> The exegesis of the church of old was based on two presuppositions: first, that the gospels contain a history; and second, that this history was a super-natural one. Rationalism rejected the second of these presuppositions, but only in order to hang on more tenaciously to the first, insisting that these books present plain, though only natural, history. Science cannot remain satisfied with this half-measure. The other presupposition must also be given up, and the investigation must first be made whether in fact, and to what extent, the ground on which we stand in the Gospels is historical.

This seems to be a straightforward capitulation to science. But Strauss, of course, was more subtle. Science may have the right to adjudicate on the truth or otherwise of factual propositions, and facts may have to be the foundation of truth. But there is more to life, and the meaning of life, than science. There is also the world of myth.

The word 'myth' in the nineteenth century had not become synonymous with 'false', as it has for us. The concept and the evaluation of myth has in fact had a very long history, during which its virtues and limitations have been threshed out – when, for example, the Romans had to take over the myths of the Greeks; when Christians had to evaluate the myths of Rome; when the pagan gods rose from the dead during the Renaissance; and above all in the nineteenth century, when myth, positively understood, offered the great opportunity to claim that truth can be told as much through fiction as through scientific fact (think how much the novel developed during this century), as much through a poem as through a mathematical proof – indeed, more so, because, as Schelling put it, mythology goes beyond the new physics: 'What is every beautiful mythology', he asked, 'but a hieroglyphic expression of surrounding nature in a transfiguration of imagination and love?'

It is that positive understanding of myth which Strauss brought to bear on the Gospels. He seized on Hegel's distinction between 'idea' and 'fact', with 'idea' being transcendence of the fact in the direction of meaning. Religions are the great communities of 'meaning-making', or, to use Strauss's own term, of 'myth-making'. Pure myth may have no connection with any event, but equally, myth may arise from events in order to draw out their meaning. Events are not left 'back there' in the past as bare happenings. They are given meaning. So when Strauss called attention to the primary role of myth in relation to Jesus, he was not denying that there were facts and events which had happened. He was rejecting the approach which tries to sort out scientifically which facts are factual, and which then discards everything else as useless fiction, or as worthless invention. Clearly something happened in the case of Jesus. But what is more important? The archaeology which attempts to establish the certain details of his biography (which are *in fact* extremely few)? Of course not. Far more important for us, according to Strauss, is to understand the way in which the followers of Jesus used the mythological opportunities of their Bible to convey his significance and importance for them.

It was this relation of myth to meaning which created the possibility of a braver new world than the one which Aldous Huxley was later to imagine as a consequence of science. It is a world just as real as that of science, but it is independent from it. It is that world of poetry and passion which Arthur Elliott lost (p. 104) when he thought it could only be found in the religion of his day: it is the aesthetic world to which Blake and Coleridge were early guides. *Aesthetica* was the title of a book by Baumgarten which had appeared in 1750. He had argued that the purpose of a work of art is not to portray or reflect reality, nor even to teach moral lessons or give pleasure. Its purpose, the aesthetic end in itself, is, as he put it, 'the perfection of sensuous cognition, . . . that is, beauty'. A poet is the creator (*poietes*) of another world, or, to put together two Greek words, as Baumgarten did put them together, poetry is *heterocosmic*: it creates and deals with another world than the one we live in when we study the laws of nature; it cannot therefore be assessed for truth by the same criteria, but only by such criteria as self-consistency and internal coherence, and thus by its capacity to deliver that satisfaction to which we give the name 'beauty'.

This was the first step toward that ultimate resistance to mechanistic scientism which is summarized at the end of the nineteenth century in the figure of Oscar Wilde, and in the phrase, 'Art for art's sake'; and that in turn is the elucidation of Kant's claim, in *The Critique of Judgement*, that a work of beauty is experienced as an end in itself, by an act of judgement which

is what it is in relation to such a work, an act which is entirely
free from any consideration of the reality or the utility of the
object. That is why A. C. Bradley could entitle his inaugural lecture at Oxford, 'Poetry for Poety's Sake', and could argue that
the experience of poetry is an end in itself – or, as the critic
I. A. Richards was later to put it, a poem must be judged by what
it is, not by what it says.

So for Bradley the purpose of poetry is not to be

> a part, nor yet a copy of the real world, . . . but to be a world
> by itself, independent, complete, autonomous; and to possess
> it fully you must enter that world, conform to its laws, and
> ignore for the time the beliefs, aims and particular conditions
> which belong to you in the other world of reality.

It then makes sense to press the aesthetic point further and
regard music as the supreme form of art, since no matter how
much nineteenth-century music might be programmatic –
Berlioz, Tchaikovsky, Liszt, and so on – music might more obviously be about nothing but itself – hence the famous conclusion
of one of the greatest aesthetes of them all, Walter Pater (he of
whom Thomas Hardy said, when he met him, that his manner
was 'that of one carrying weighty ideas about without spilling
them'), 'All art aspires to the condition of music.'

This is the autonomy of art in distinction from science. It
creates its own world in relation to beauty, through its reliance
on the sheer quality of human feelings and ideals. It is these
which create the idiosyncratic worlds which humans inhabit in
their heads, and to these 'other worlds' Newtonian mechanists
can gain no access. The virtue of poetry is that it is immune to
the virus of science, in a way that religion is not, because religion is entangled in claims about putative matters of fact; and
that is exactly the context of the passage quoted earlier from
Matthew Arnold about the failure of the religious fact:

> The future of poetry is immense, because in poetry, where it
> is worthy of its high destinies, our race, as time goes on, will
> find an ever surer and surer stay. There is not a creed which
> is not shaken, not an accredited dogma which is not shown to
> be questionable, not a received tradition which does not
> threaten to dissolve. Our religion has materialised itself in
> the fact, in the supposed fact; it has attached its emotion to
> the fact, and now the fact is failing it. But for poetry the idea

is everything; the rest is a world of illusion, of divine illusion. Poetry attaches its emotion to the idea; the idea is the fact. The strongest part of our religion today is its unconscious poetry.

In this spirit, it is not surprising that Newman regarded poetry as the antagonist of science and the corresponding hope for religion:

> Poetry, then, I conceive, whatever be its metaphysical essence, or however various may be its kinds, . . . poetry is always the antagonist to *science*. . . . Poetry does not address the reason, but the imagination and affections; it leads to admiration, enthusiasm, devotion, love. Hence it is that a child's mind is so full of poetry, because he knows so little [remember Reade?]. That is why the savage is more poetical than the citizen, the knight errant than the brigadier-general, the winding bridle-path than the straight railroad, the ruin than the spruce suburban box, the Turkish robe or Spanish doublet than the French dress coat.[15]

But where, in the nineteenth century, might one have seen people dressed in a Turkish robe or a Spanish doublet? In, of course, an opera. And now we see why people went unfed to *Parsifal* as to a Holy Communion (before which it was still a matter of discipline at this time to eat nothing for some hours). It was a religious act. All that we have been tracing so far makes the ambition and the programme of Wagner intelligible – one might almost say, inevitable. If Wagner had not existed, the romantic resistance movement of the nineteenth century would have had to invent him. Wagner is the consummation and the epitome of this resistance movement to the territorial ambitions of science in the nineteenth century. For it was Wagner who took poetry and myth to the furthest possible extreme, and who believed that the vocation of the artist is to produce, in relation to myth, what he called 'the total work of art'.

What Wagner meant by the 'total art work' is most clearly described in *The Artwork of the Future*. To quote Max Nordau's (admittedly antagonistic) summary:

> The fundamental thought of the *Artwork of the Future* is this: the first and most original of the arts was that of dancing; its peculiar essence is rhythm, and this has developed into music; music, consisting of rhythm and tone, has raised

(Wagner says 'condensed') its phonetic element to speech, and produced the art of poetry; the highest form of poetry is the drama, which for the purpose of stage construction, and to imitate the natural scene of human action, has associated itself with architecture and painting respectively; finally, sculpture is nothing but the giving permanence to the appearance of the actor in a dead rigid form, while acting is real sculpture in living, flowing movement. Thus all the arts group themselves around the drama, and the latter should unite them naturally. Nevertheless they appear at present in isolation, to the great injury of each and of art in general. This reciprocal estrangement and isolation of the different arts is an unnatural and decadent condition, and the effort of true artists must be to win them back to their natural and necessary conjunction with each other. The mutual penetration and fusion of all arts into a single art will produce the genuine work of art. Hence the work of art of the future is a drama with music and dance, which unrolls itself in a landscape painting, has for a frame a masterly creation of architectural art designed for the poetico-musical end, and is represented by actors who are really sculptors, but who realise their plastic inspirations by means of their own bodily appearance.

True to his text, Wagner composed both words and music of his works, including *Parsifal*, and involved himself closely in the design, not only of the sets and costumes, but also of the auditorium itself at Bayreuth. He called Parsifal *Buhnenweihfestspiel*, which might be translated (as it often is) 'sacred festival drama', but in fact is more accurately translated (in relation to Wagner's own intentions), 'festival work to consecrate a stage' – the stage being Bayreuth, and the consecration being for the continuity of Wagner's work.

Wagner did not deny that science has a limited truth to tell, because it is a consequence of what he called, in *The Music of the Future*, 'the ineradicable quality of the human perceptive process, which impelled man to the discovery of the laws of causality, and because of which he involuntarily asks himself, in the face of every impressive phenomenon – "Why is this?".' Far from disappearing into an abstraction of music from the real world in order to produce pure beauty, Wagner argued that the total work of art returns the spectator *to* the real world, and offers much richer answers to the question, 'Why?':

The drama, at the moment of its realistic, scenic presentation awakens in the spectator real participation in the action presented to him; and this is so faithfully imitated from real life (or at least from the possibilities of it), that the sympathetic human feeling passes through such participation into a state of ecstasy which forgets that momentous question 'Why?' and willingly yields itself up to the guidance of those new laws through which music makes itself so strangely intelligible and at the same time – in the deepest sense – gives the only correct answer to that 'Why?'

So there are other and, humanly speaking, far more important questions than physics can possibly answer. What questions? Wagner's operas are the answer. But take *Parsifal*, as an example: the questions are obviously those of suffering and sin: Why do people suffer? How are their sufferings related both to their own past and to the far larger story in which their lives are caught up? And how can we be redeemed from the past? Why does Kundry both help and hinder, the latter often against her will – *Ich helfe nie* (I give no help) she cries scornfully to Gurnemanz (i.1.144); why does Amfortas turn his face to the wall, begging Titurel to resume his role [*Wehe! Wehe mir der Qual! / Mein Vater, oh! noch einmal / verrichte du das Amt! / Lebe, leb und lass mich sterben,*[16] (i.2.26-9)], and yet he presides at the grail ceremony for the knights? Three times, when Parsifal makes his first appearance, he says, *Das weiss ich nicht* (i.1.285ff.), (I do not know).

A Newtonian in the nineteenth century would have had confidence that at least in theory he could have answered the question, why has the past brought the present into its present form of existence? He would have thought that a theoretical knowledge of the position and momentum of all the atoms of the universe would have enabled a prediction of all future states. But can we re-enter the past? Agathon, according to Aristotle, had said, 'This only is denied, even to God: the power to undo the past.' Myth, above all the Christian myth of a Redeemer, allows even that to God. And that is Wagner's question which physics cannot answer: how can we be redeemed from the past? How can we, so to speak, re-enter the past and find forgiveness for the harm and the damage we have done? Gurnemanz on Titurel: *unkund blieb mir, was dorten er gesundigt, / doch welt er bussen nun, ja heilig werden*[17] (i.1.201f.); Kundry to Parsifal: *Bekenntnis / wird Schuld in Reue enden, / Erkenntnis / in*

Sinn die Torheit wenden[18] (ii.358-61); Amfortas longing for the knights to bring him, not the Grail but death, which might be 'a small atonement for a sin like mine' (iii.249). And unifying these glimpses of redemption is the concept and the action of what Wagner in *Parsifal* calls *Mitleid*, or, elsewhere in his other writings, *Mitleiden*.

Mitleid is usually translated 'pity' but more literally it means 'suffering with', *com-passio*. Parsifal does not merely pity Amfortas: he enters without evasion into his suffering and shares it, and in that bearing of the same suffering begins to acquire the self-knowledge and the self-understanding which he has previously lacked and which therefore impede his own redemption; and it is Kundry's kiss – an action of *mitleid* – which awakens Parsifal to the reality of suffering. That is the single quality of the long-awaited redeemer:

> Before the wrecked sanctuary
> Amfortas lay in fervent prayer,
> Begging a sign of pardon.
> A mystic light illuminated the Grail;
> A holy vision appeared to him and spoke . . . :
>> Made wise through *mitleid*
>> The blameless simpleton,
>> Wait for him,
>> The one I choose. (I.i.234ff.);

and these are exactly the words central to the Grail scene itself, Act I, scene 2.

These themes are clearly close to those of Christianity. It might seem to be the case, therefore, that a Wagnerian response to science puts an oblique version of a Christian theme on stage and makes myth a substitute for mass. But Wagner has moved far beyond anything so naïve. It is a common question to ask whether *Parsifal* is a Christian work. Superficially it may seem that it is. Wagner himself wrote of *Parsifal* in answer to his patron Ludwig's question, 'Why did it take the kiss of Kundry to convert Parsifal?', with a direct appeal to the Christian myth of the Fall:

You know the serpent in Paradise with its beguiling promise, *eritis sicut Deus scientes bonum et malum*. Adam and Eve became 'knowing'. They became knowingly aware of sin. The human race had to atone for that consciousness by suffering both shame and misery, until it was redeemed by Christ, when he took upon himself the sins of the world.

So are we, after all this, to conclude that *Parsifal* is fundamentally a Christian work? But by now we have seen that the question is not answerable because it is not even 'askable'. To think that one can even ask the question is to have misunderstood the whole of the nineteenth century. It is a confusion of categories. Certainly the Christian myth is present, but so are Greek myths, Grimm's tales, Buddhism as mediated by Schopenhauer, Nordic icons. It is possible to see *Parsifal* as a Christian work if you wish to do so: it contains Good Friday, the Grail, the spear that wounded the side of the redeemer, and the redeemer himself. Lucy Beckett argues that *Parsifal* is Christian, and so indeed did Nietzsche, although in outrage that Wagner had sold his soul to such a devil. In a new Preface to *Human, All too Human*, which he wrote in 1886, he wrote that Wagner 'suddenly sank down, helpless and broken, before the Christian cross'.

But others have protested, on more general grounds, that *Parsifal* is not a Christian work. Michael Ascham takes eleven separate points where some Christian connection might be made and argues, either that they have more pagan (or non-Christian) connections that they do Christian, or that Christian imagery is used but not imitated.[19] Michael Tanner argues that *Parsifal* is anti-Christian, at least in the sense that it is designed to exhibit 'the psychopathology of religious belief in artistic terms'.[20]

From Wagner himself, it is not possible to derive an answer, because he said both 'Yes' and 'No' – partly, one suspects, according to what he thought a particular person wanted to hear: Wagner was often in desperate financial straits. Thus he wrote to his patron King Ludwig, 'It seems to me as though I have been inspired to undertake this work in order to sustain for the world its inherent, most profound mystery – the truest Christian faith, indeed, to awaken this faith anew.'[21]

But in truth, *Parsifal* cannot be 'a Christian work', because to speak in those terms is to miss the point: it is a work, not about Christianity, but about us; and if Christianity, or Buddhism, or Nordic myths, or Grimm's fairy tales are 'about us', then they lend themselves to any true answer to the questions of 'Why?' which we ask about ourselves. In this way, religious truth, or rather the truths which religions may have preserved in the past, are immune from sceptical or positivistic attack. The scientist may understand the world, it is the simpleton who redeems it.

Wagner is the extreme consequence of this antagonistic understanding of the relation between science and religion. It may seem far removed from that competition of causes which left room for God only in the gaps. Finding a few remaining gaps for God had been seen very early, at least by those who were wise, to be the conversion of God into the grin of the Cheshire cat. But surely in the deep green wood with Arthur Elliott (p. 104), surely at night beneath the glorious starlit sky, not just with Elliott but also with Kant, one might find a comparably impregnable ground which transcendental humans might call their own?

> When I heard the learn'd astronomer,
> When the proofs, the figures, were ranged in columns
>   before me,
> When I was shown the charts and diagrams, to add, divide,
>   and measure them,
> When I sitting heard the astronomer where he lectured
>   with much applause in the lecture room,
> How soon unaccountable I became tired and sick,
> Till rising and gliding out I wander'd off by myself,
> In the mystical moist night-air, and from time to time,
> Look'd up in perfect silence at the stars.[22]

Yet all this was leading nowhere, because it was in truth only a variation on the same evasive theme: Wagner may have avoided the issue of the God of the gaps, but what he and others were seeking was a man of the gaps, an account of humanity the truth of which could not be questioned or claimed by science. On their account, religions may have preserved this in the past, but they are now too compromised (by their attachment to falsified facts) to do so in the present.

At the time when Wagner was writing, one other strategy on the part of religion was to retreat into the past, into a world of religious emotion and poetry which 'premythologizes' the facts and equates them with mystery. It remains a favourite strategy, as one can see in the many forms of fundamentalism from the Vatican to the suburbs of Tokyo. In the nineteenth century, it was this strategy which produced the Gothic revival – of which Leslie Stephen was in fact writing when he used that phrase of God as a *roi fainéant*, a constitutional king (p. 102); and he pointed out exactly why it was bound to fail:

> We have succeeded in building churches so carefully modelled after the old patterns, that William of Wykeham might rise from the dead and fancy that his old architects were at work. . . . There is only one objection to our complete success. The more skilfully we imitate obsolete modes of art or religion the more palpably dead they become.[23]

Wagner saw the point exactly, and therefore, while he drew on myths from any religion which served his purpose, it was not in order to revive them, but in order to produce a new mythology, a new religion, a myth fit for our times. He concluded – as did so many, even, against all expectation, Weber – that we need a new formulation of religion. In a late work, *Religion and Art*, Wagner wrote:

> One could say that at the point where religion becomes artificial it is for art to preserve the essence of religion by grasping the symbolic value of its mythic symbols, which the former would have us believe in their literal sense, so that the deep, hidden truth in them might be revealed by their ideal representatives.

This, then, is the context for our own explorations of the relation between science and religion. We have inherited this division between scientific and symbolic uses of language, between objective description and subjective experience. Science is taken to be more enduringly true than religion because it is empirically based on observation and repeatable experiment. Science progresses through time, accumulating knowledge and perhaps (if we are fallibilistic absolutists) aspiring to a complete account of all that is genuinely knowable. Religion, on this account, must give way to science, because its own claims about putative matters of fact have been so repeatedly falsified. Religion has therefore retreated into symbol and art as the expression of personal and social experience. Inevitably, therefore, religion is committed to metaphorical language, and if it is theistic, it espouses metaphorical theology. Where science is objective, descriptive and representational, religion is subjective and allusive, creating communities of shared symbols through which the meanings and aspirations of our lives can be expressed. But knowledge it is not.

This is the agenda that we have inherited, and it still dominates the scene. You only have to pick up a book by Dawkins to see that. But what would happen if we refuse the agenda?

What would happen if we look at the relationship or interaction between science and religion in an entirely different way? The relationship looks entirely different when one realizes that the more comprehensive and persistent issue between religions and science has been one, not of propositions, but of power. Who has the right and the authority, the rewards and the sanctions, which allow them to determine what may and may not happen in human life? Where do the dispositions of authority, control and power lie – at one extreme over the universe, but more locally and more immediately, over human affairs?

The two are, of course, very closely related. The authority of that which is claimed to control order, form and process in the cosmos (however the cosmos is perceived and imagined) is mediated into the control and ordering of society and of individual lives, not least through the authority figures which exist in any social system. The linkage between the two is more obvious in religious systems, because of the relative clarity of their boundaries. But even in the more diffuse systems of a modern political economy, it is not hard to see the ways in which those who espouse the paradigmatic primacy of science seek to translate this into the ordering of society – for example, in the allocation of priorities in public expenditure, or in education. An even more extreme example is that of sociobiology, discussed at length in my *Is God a Virus?* If science describes nature as the authority and power under which we all necessarily live, then humans to be wise must understand nature better and adapt their lives to her law.

That view is pervasive. It has been combined in the post-Enlightenment centuries with a belief and a campaign that religions no longer have any *right* (and the word 'rights' has itself been prominent) to maintain control over lives and societies other than those of their own constituency; and for sure, religion should mind its own business and not interfere in politics. The rise of science and the advance of technology demonstrate an authority and mediate a new power of control which is independent of religious construction.

This can hardly be welcome news for those religious traditions which have exercised authority and control over whole societies, whether those societies are the size of a village or the size of the *oikumene* – the whole inhabited world. Religions mediate strategic decisions in the operation of human lives and in the construction of societies. The individual may be the locus of those decisions, but only in a context of religious value and approval – or sanction. This is the classic balance between conscience and authority in Christianity, to which the recent Vatican documents have returned in an attempt to redress the balance in favour of authority.

In this context, the challenge of science to religion lies in the independence of its own authority and of its sources of control. Nature can be encountered and studied outside the boundaries of religious authority and control, and the consequences of that study are of effect without the benefit of clergy. The issue is epitomised in the nineteenth-century work of William Farr, who wrote in *Vital Statistics* (Part 4):

> The great source of misery of mankind is not their numbers, but their imperfections, and the want of control over the conditions in which they live ... There is a definite task before us – to determine from observation the sources of Health, and the direct causes of death in the two sexes at different ages and under the different conditions. The exact determination of evils is the first step towards their remedies.

Science shifts the control over life and nature by research in contrast to ritual, and it remedies the evils which afflict us, not by exorcism, but by experiment. Science therefore challenges the exercise of authority and control by religions in areas where it has traditionally obtained. It is this which is the issue between science and religions, not immediately that of a conflict of propositions. There is no intrinsic reason why the propositions and practices of science cannot be accommodated by a religion. After all, the origins of science lie deeply embedded in religious beliefs and motivations. Religions have many different ways of handling propositional conflict. The ones they choose are usually strategic decisions in defence of the authority of their own world-construction – and where individuals are concerned, it is that point of world-construction which is all important. Religions are not primarily addressed to making experimental sorties in pursuit of truth; they are addressed to the questions of what a good life is and how it can be lived, and of what the end or purpose of it may be.

None of this implies that the issues of propositional truth about the cosmos are unimportant. All that I am arguing is that the issues of propositional truth are a kind of sub-text in the overall document. Of course they are important in themselves, so much so that particular debates can take on a life and a library of their own. But they are only a sub-text, in the sense that religions, or religious people, or religious leaders, have other more important interests, and can therefore deal with propositional issues in so many different ways: Ian Barbour, in *Religion in an Age of Science*, classified them into four groups, conflict, independence, dialogue and integration. But there is nothing within religion itself which determines which strategy must be adopted. What is usually the case is that the public strategy adopted by any particular religion will be a part of the much larger strategy of maintaining the authority and control of the religion in question.

This means that in any particular religion there may well be a number of different strategies going on at once, and certainly there will be changes in strategy as the years go by. On the 350th anniversary of the publication of Galileo's *Dialogues*, Pope John Paul II observed that there had been developed 'a more accurate appreciation of the methods proper to the different orders of knowledge': 'It is only through humble and assiduous study that she [the Church] learns to dissociate the essentials of faith from the scientific systems of a given age, especially when a culturally influenced reading of the Bible seemed to be linked to an obligatory cosmology.'[24] Yet this is the same religious system which is still maintaining in its official teaching that 'death makes its entrance into human history' only as a consequence of the disobedience of Adam and Eve (*Catechism of the Catholic Church*, 397–400). An obligatory anthropology has been substituted for an obligatory cosmology, and in this instance the strategy of 350 years ago is still being adopted in one while it is being repudiated in the other.

In contrast to that confusion, how do I see the relation of science and religion and the agenda of work to be done? Given that I understand religion as being both the practice and the consequence of somatic exploration,[25] then of course the relationship is obvious: it is one of opportunity. Both science and religion belong to the enterprise of exploration, though by no means of the same subject-matter by the same methods. To think that would be a grievous error. But both arise from the nature of the human animal to explore that nature and the environment in which it is set. Both make discoveries which endure through time: in both cases they achieve reliability, though always they are open to correction and change. No doubt many religious people refuse to change or be changed and lapse into an incoherence in relation to science in which, quite often, they rejoice. But in the long run it is of little consequence that the earth goes round the sun, rather than the reverse, since in the long run (apart from the fact that we will all be dead, a perspective which religions take seriously) all religions will find a strategy to accommodate contradictory propositions, even if only by denying them.

So I repeat the point: propositional and conceptual issues will come and go; and while they are often important, they are important only as second-order issues. Of primary concern are the issues of power, authority and control. The consequences of science are always a passing episode in human history: religions are unwise if they tie their fortunes to a sinking ship. But the methods of science endure, and at least up to the present, they adhere to one of that triad of values which religion is also called to inscribe into human life and history: truth. To that extent, religion and science ought to be natural and inevitable partners: if religions fail in that part of their vocation, then that is a far more serious threat to their future than any particular conflicts with science. It will mean that religions have opted for a strategy of irrationality in defending their authority, which is indeed what we see happening at the present time: religions are firing rockets against reason (sometimes, oddly, in the name of something called post-modernism).

We are all involved in the consequences of this, whether we are religious or not. In my view, money would be better spent exploring this issue, rather than the particular propositional issues, to which, at the moment, because this is what 'science and religion' is taken to mean, virtually all our resources are given. We need to break the dominance of the inherited agenda. Maybe then we will recover the confidence of a Traherne, who lived, not in both worlds at once, but in both worlds as one:

> He that knows the secrets of nature with Albertus Magnus, or the motions of the heavens with Galileo, or the cosmography of the moon with Hevelius, or the body of man with Galen, or the nature of diseases with Hippocrates, or the harmonies in melody with Orpheus, or of poesie with Homer, or of grammar with Lilly, or of whatever else with the greatest artist; he is nothing if he knows them merely for talk or idle speculation, or transient and external use. But he that knows them for value, and knows them his own, shall profit infinitely. And therefore of all kinds of learnings, humanity and divinity are the most excellent.[26]

Chapter Eight

IS SCIENCE THE NEW RELIGION?

Mary Hesse

Authority and Relativism

In the previous chapter, John Bowker described an era which was essentially one of profound confidence. There was confidence about the powers of science to deliver truth about nature, and in the possibility of technological fall-out to the benefit of human life. There was even confidence about religion, in spite of all the doubts of some who saw warfare between science and religion, and in spite of the romantic reaction away from orthodox religion towards the gods of Valhalla or various types of Nietzschean anarchism. In spite of all this the authority of divine revelation and the established churches remained both intellectually respectable and acceptable to the mass of people.

We, on the other hand, live in an era of profound *scepticism*. The term 'relativism' is not only banded about by philosophers, but has become current in such down-to-earth topics as the conduct of religious education in primary schools. Relativism is the view that no one can lay claim to absolute truth (not even in science, as we shall see presently), therefore it is up to everyone to choose their allegiance, whether to the traditional authorities of their social group, Christian, Moslem, liberal humanist or whatever, or to their own perceived individual needs. All this has been fuelled by various influential intellectual movements, including Wittgenstein's internally coherent and self-sufficient language games, and the studies of diverse exotic societies in social anthropology which seemed to exemplify them so well. Even in the discipline of history there were emphases on studying the past from the point of view of its contemporary actors, without Whiggish judgements about their, to us, naïve beliefs and outlandish moral systems.

Combined with our own persisting traditions of liberal individualism, this has produced some strange contradictions. Sharp distinctions are made between the public and the private. As far as public policy is concerned we believe in the power and responsibilities of social groups; the coherence of the family having largely broken down, we look to social services, national institutions and ultimately to governments to solve all social problems, and to take corresponding blame when things go wrong. But as far as the private and personal is concerned, modes of life are nobody's business but our own and those we choose to associate with. Liberty is increasingly controlled in public by the bureaucratic state, but increasingly becomes licence in private. We are profoundly sceptical of authority, in spite of relying upon it in many areas of life, and at the same time profoundly individualistic, trusting only our own reasonings and desires.

It does not take much historical insight to see that this is an essentially unstable state of affairs. There is tension between the extremes of social order and increasing authority on the one hand, and the tendency to social disruption and anarchy on the other. Both these states of affairs can be traced in various ways back to the intellectual fall-out of successful natural science.

A gloomy diagnosis. I begin like this because I want to relate what I have to say about science as a potential new religion to John Bowker's suggestion that the nineteenth-century debate about science and religion ought to be seen as a struggle of powers and authorities. Although Marxism as a political creed is currently, and rightly, having a hard time, we should not forget that we owe to it a far more realistic insight into the workings of power in human society than anything produced by the post-Enlightenment liberals and rationalists.

What has all this to do with the relations of science and religion? My title is 'Is Science the New Religion?'. This is intended to draw attention to the possibility that religion, in spite of its present decline, has essential functions in human life for which it is widely agreed some replacement must be found. So the questions of power and authority are crucial: what has the authority to replace religion? Some cling to increasingly fundamentalist versions of traditional religions; some look to social and political ideologies; but more often in the liberal, rationalist tradition of the West, it is science that is the prime candidate – science taken in the broadest sense to include the social and psychological as well as the physical and biological sciences.

So what I want to look at is the nature of the authority claimed by science in general. There is no doubt of course about its *power*. This is inherent in the technology without which modern society would collapse, with all its negative as well as positive features, and the immense vested interests involved. But it is not about technological power I want to write, but rather about rational authority. In a prophetic prevision of our current dilemmas, Kant asked three different and fundamental philosophical questions, to which he proceeded to give three different types of answer. '*What can we know?*': what we can know, he said, in that century after Newton, was science, the product of the pure reason, producing truths about the natural world, most strikingly in his time about 'the starry skies above'. '*What though, should we do?*'; to this he answered in terms of what he called 'practical reason', 'the moral law within'. He appealed to the concept of duty, which he thought was essentially innate in the human psyche, as he also thought (wrongly) the principles of science are. His third question, '*What can we hope for?*', concerns the ends and purposes of life and the world. Here he gave the arts and religion their place. His replies to the second and third questions are less satisfactory than those to the first and less discussed, and the possibility of even asking them has been comparatively neglected in subsequent philosophy. But they do not go away, and now is the time for the analysis of science and religion to take account of them.

To take Kant's first question first. Obviously we know a great deal more from three or four centuries of modern science than we knew before, and the success of technology shows this conclusively. But when philosophers and theologians look at science it is not this kind of scientific knowledge they are interested in. Karl Popper built his whole philosophy of science on a dismissal of the intellectual importance of scientific technology – what he called pure instrumentalism – and concentrated on what science tells us about the true and deep structure of the natural world. That is what science seeks, but paradoxically according to Popper that is not what we can finally have, all we can know is what natural reality is *not* like. Our theories must be logically capable of being falsified by subsequent experience, but they can never be conclusively confirmed as true. Nevertheless he elevated this endless will-o'-the-wisp of scientific truth to being the ultimate purpose and motivation of all science – Truth and nothing but Truth. Others less subtle and clear-sighted than

Popper have claimed that we can reach Truth in science, or at least that we can get nearer and nearer to it so that effectively we arrive. And some of these truths they claim we can arrive at have important relevance to how we understand the world and our place in it, and therefore they appear to be in the same ball-park as religion.

God in Modern Cosmology

First I shall take some examples from modern cosmology – the study of the furthest reaches of Kant's starry skies above. There have recently been several books and articles by physical cosmologists who have become household names; Stephen Hawking,[1] Paul Davies,[2] John Barrow,[3] Frank Tipler.[4] They are authors of titles like *A Brief History of Time, The Mind of God, Theories of Everything.* In these there are suggestions for a new God – a God who (or which) is essentially the structure of the laws of nature itself, conceived as universal and eternal, independent of human knowledge, and encompassing all possible knowledge. These, it is suggested, have already largely been discovered in the latest theories of physics, astronomy and cosmology, and we can be confident in their essential truth. Translated into theological terms, this structure of laws is said to have the properties of omnipotence, absoluteness and omniscience, all of which are traditional attributes of the deity. Thus, according for example to Paul Davies, it becomes possible to discuss many of the perennial problems about the universe that have traditionally been the province of religion; how and when it began, what will be its fate, whether it is designed, what is the significance of its beauty and orderliness. It also makes it possible to celebrate the god-like powers humans must possess to have been able to penetrate it, and their apparent moral duty to pursue all these natural truths as far as the mind can take them.

There is no doubt that there is great fascination and excitement among the educated public about these metaphysical and theological sounding claims. It is easy to see why, given pervading scepticism about traditional religious answers to questions about the meaning and value of the world, and given that science has appeared the only successful way of answering them. 'Lord to whom shall we go, thou hast the words of eternal life', but it is science that has them, not the Lord Jesus.

It may seem churlish to try to debunk these glowing visions, resting as they do on such brilliant exercise of intellectual power and imagination. But in the interests of a better understanding of what is required of a religion, it must be done.

First let me compare a few quotations from the cosmologists. In his book entitled *Theories of Everything,* John Barrow says

> Science is predicated upon the belief that ... there is an abbreviated representation of the logic behind the Universe's properties that can be written down in finite form by human beings, *and* the modern search for a Theory of Everything is the ultimate expression of that belief.[5]

In spite of this strong statement, however, Barrow in the same book makes it clear that 'Everything' does not mean 'everything' – it does not mean every particular property and event in the world; the hairs of our heads are not all numbered. In other words it leaves out everything that intimately concerns human life and history. The presence of a particular star and one of its planets upon which life could evolve, the detailed course of that evolution, not to speak of the two-legged mammals and their history down to the calculating minds of cosmologists, all these are *accidents* relative to the rational logic of the underlying mathematical structure which is somehow identified in these cosmologists' writings with the Mind of God. There is a contrast of mathematical, impersonal order, which is the only context given to the concept of God, with the messy, dynamic, contingent and accidental history of the universe and humankind, which apparently has no place for God. Quite apart from the question of whether the cosmological theories are actually true, the consequences of this lop-sided emphasis are culturally profound.

But first we should ask whether such an absolute and pervasive mathematical order does indeed exist in any form that we can be certain of having discovered? The Astronomer Royal, Martin Rees, is much more modest in his claims. In a recent lecture he warned the Association for Science Education that cosmologists are not to be taken seriously when they speculate about the universe in the first second after the Big Bang. We can go back to plus one second with fairly well-supported and understood physics, but earlier than that physics itself is under test. But it is just the first few micro-seconds that cosmologists appeal to when they claim to address metaphysical-sounding questions about the ultimate lawfulness of the universe, and its origins and destiny. Even the existence of the Big Bang itself depends on the extrapolation of physics back to the very beginning. In other words the shaky place given to religious concepts in many of the popular cosmologists is not based on sound science. Paul Davies (author of *The Mind of God*) would, I think, agree with Martin Rees here, but if so the importance he goes on to ascribe to science reads a little strangely. He expresses the view that

> the fact that science works so well, points to something profoundly significant about the organization of the cosmos. Any attempt to understand the nature of reality and the place of human beings in the universe must proceed from a sound scientific base.

Why, in light of the fact that our most fundamental theories are never totally reliable and always subject to revolutionary change? Why are such temporary imaginative models of the world important for anything else than their function in natural science itself, which is to help us organize and make use of the low-level laws that we find solidly based in experiment? That function of science does not in any sense justify grand metaphysical claims for theories. But perhaps it is unfair to judge the significance of science in general from cosmology, which is a special case in being as far removed from and sparsely supported by the here-and-now evidence as any theories can be. In case this may be so, we can look briefly at another type of science where quasi-metaphysical claims have been made for its fundamental theories, namely evolutionary biology.

The theory of evolution has been used to support either of two conflicting views of the existence of purpose in nature. Either evolution is held to reveal an underlying purposive principle, culminating in the human reason which can understand so much of its workings; or the theory is held to prove the absence of any such evidence of design. Unlike physics, biological theory does introduce the concepts of real time, with the dynamics of contingently evolving futures, full of unpredictable possibilities. This is at least a scenario more conducive to an understanding of human fortunes than the static logic of a mathematical physics. But most biologists would deny the presence of any ultimate meaning or purpose within this process. There is indeed marvellous design packed, for example, into the DNA of the first cells of the embryo, and in the incredibly

complex interdependence of an ecological system. But these
have always constituted for biologists a challenge to find non-
purposive explanations, and the history of recent biological
theory has been one of successful response to such challenges.
Darwin's theory of natural selection, and the more recent top-
down causation postulated, for example, in complex organic
systems and electronic simulations of mind, seem to have eliminated any need for extra-biological sources of design. Even if
this is too quick a rejection of intrinsic purpose, it must also
be noted that such purpose would have to accommodate less
desirable features; nature red in tooth and claw, epidemics, starvation and premature death. Far from looking like benevolent
design, these natural phenomena have always been regarded as
aspects of the intractable problem of evil which stands in the
way of belief in any benevolent God. The problem of evil would
always be untouched by any evidences of purpose in biology.

An Ethic of Science?

These are only two examples of the attempts to discuss metaphysics and theology within natural science, and they indicate
that nothing like the traditional concept of a God can be found
there. But does the attempt to escape from relativism by means
of the authority of science actually need such metaphysical
concepts? I shall argue later that it does, but meanwhile the
possibility must be considered that perhaps science itself, as a
way of life and a methodical ethos, rather than a body of
knowledge, should be sufficient in a truly modern society. We
may be able to do without God, but most would agree that, as
individuals and societies, we cannot do without value-systems.

There is of course an ancient philosophical maxim according
to which 'Ought cannot be derived from Is'. If science is about
facts, then values and moral systems cannot be derived from
science. But this is perhaps a too rapid rejection of the idea of
a 'scientific ethic'. Science is not entirely about facts. For a start,
the practice of science demands a disciplined attention to
experiments to confirm or refute theories, a willingness to
collaborate with other scientists whose care and honesty has to
be relied upon, and a persistent regard for truths of logic and
experiment even when they seem to contradict our best-loved
theories. Is this 'ethic of science' sufficient for the conduct of
a life? It is undoubtedly valuable, but surely not enough. It is

largely a historical product of a slightly utopian concept of the human being according to which liberal values of regard for truth, tolerance of others' opinions, the capacity for rational argument, and a basic trust of other people's goodwill is regarded as a sufficient response to life's problems. The extent of current disillusionment with the whole public political world is a measure of our persisting adherence to this optimistic consensus in face of all experience to the contrary. The poor may or may not be always with us, but the corrupt certainly are.

A life primarily devoted to science is often able to bypass these truths of interhuman relations. Philip Oppenheimer memorably brought this to light after the use of the atomic bombs in 1945, when he exclaimed 'now science has known sin'. Nothing in the prevailing 'ethic of science' had prepared those physicists for the agonizing dilemmas of whether to work on, or to use, the atomic bomb in the circumstances of that time. The observable facts of evil are not solvable problems to be eliminated by scientific methods, they are endemic in the human condition. The undoubtedly important technical functions of natural science have been bought at the price of bypassing understanding of most of the other important areas of life.

It is for reasons like this that most of the traditional disputes about science and religion are entirely beside the point. They presuppose that there were some factual errors in religion, which science has corrected: the creation of the world in six days, an original male/female pair created independently of the animals, the sun goes round the earth, the existence of human free will, the possibility of miracles violating the laws of nature, or of the resurrection of a man from the dead. These things are indeed deeply problematic and they do reveal factual inconsistencies between some traditions of science and religion, but to start there is to assume that natural science has something decisive to say about their religious significance. That is not the place to start. The place to start is rather to ask Kant's other two questions; *What should we do?*; *What can we hope for?* Or rather, to start by looking again at the phenomenon of religion, which in all recorded human history has spoken about these questions. It is a form of scientific hubris to suppose that we can neglect what was so long established among our predecessors.

Myths, Models and Metaphors

What, then, is a religion? Almost every recorded society has
had a socially established system of myths, beliefs, values, social
rituals and practices, usually highly symbolic, using heightened
'poetic' forms of language, often calling upon some extra-natural
reality, God or the gods. These systems have had important
social functions, in creating coherence within groups, sometimes alongside prophetic critique of some of its practices, and
interpretations for every individual of their place in the world,
both natural and supernatural.

Many of these characteristics are the very opposite of those
of science, and none more so than the appeal to extra-natural
reality, and the language of myth and symbolism that has always
been required to express it. Whenever religion has attempted
to accommodate itself to what the seventeenth-century scientists
call the 'plain, naked, natural way of speaking', religion has lost
its distinctive character and function as religion. But it is still
felt that the most damning thing that can be said about religious assertions is that they are 'mythical'. Because of the post-
Enlightenment obsession with science, the term 'myth', usually
qualified by the word 'merely', remains one of the most misunderstood in the language.

There was a recent headlined report (by a science journalist),
'Exodus and Moses merely myths, say researchers', followed by
an account of how archaeologists and historians had combed
the Egyptian records and its desert, and found no evidence
relating to a mass departure of the Israelites, nor any large-scale
disaster to Pharaoh's army in the Red Sea. The report went on,
'Other scholars, says this week's *Time* magazine, insist that the
story of the Exodus was a political fabrication to unite the
disparate tribes in Canaan through a falsified heroic past.' If
that is so, of course, the Israelites were not alone. Every society,
during perhaps a few millennia BCE and the first millennium
and more CE, has its sagas and its heroes, generally related to
an established religion. Did Arthur exist, or Alfred burn the
cakes? And of course we can give examples almost up to our
own time.

Can we take religion seriously when it is permeated by such
mythical and ideological stories, not only about wars and heroes,
but about the activities of a God or gods, which of course is
what the Exodus story is really about, and why Christians, Jews

and Moslems continue to read it? The metaphorical and mythical language of religion is perhaps nowadays the most intractable stumbling-block in the confrontation between science and religion, closely followed by the assumption exemplified by *Time* magazine just quoted, that religion has to do with telling false stories in the interests of ruling classes, of the dominance of one society over another, or just of maintaining social stability and morale.

It is useful to start a tentative approach to the more theoretical issue of the nature of religious language by noting that *science also has its myths* and is pervaded by metaphorical language. As I have indicated in the case of currently popular theories of cosmology, theories taken beyond what is warranted by the experimental basis themselves take on the social functions of myth, and can be used to wield social power. Like religions, these theories require metaphorical rather than literal language in order to express the *unobservable.* They are always interpretations of the observable in terms of some model of nature carrying its own metaphysical overtones. Think of Aristotle's closed world of turning spheres, with the earth at the privileged centre, which is modelled in the medieval astrolabes, and which had such influential intellectual and political effects in the geocentric disputes of the sixteenth and seventeenth centuries. World models at the current frontiers of physics and cosmology are not different in principle: they fit the data into a simplified narrative, stretching the ordinary use of language to suggest possible further developments which are sometimes successful and sometimes not, and when they are not, one narrative has to be replaced by another in what Kuhn called a 'scientific revolution'.

Consider the 'mechanical world' universally accepted within science for two centuries between, roughly, Newton and Maxwell. The model of the world as nothing but the collisions and push-pull of matter was not only falsely believed to be the last word of truth about nature, but also had profound human implications. It seemed to be in conflict with human rationality and freedom (Descartes' problem), it appeared to rule out so-called 'arbitrary' interventions of the deity within the world, and in general it threatened to reduce the human to the machine. Human beings become 'economic men', or *Homo sociologicus*, to be codified and experimented upon like atoms and guinea-pigs. It cuts us off from an understanding of history. Human history becomes bunk, the scene of benighted ignorance of scientific truth, of witchcraft, magic and mythology, into which dustbin religion is also dumped.

The response ran into the classic dilemmas of science and religion: either scientific materialism with no place at all for religion, except perhaps as a social and psychological prop or opium, or a dualism in which religion was banished to a realm of the supernatural and the individual soul. In either case, the task of understanding how knowledge of nature is related to human life has been abandoned to dogmatic ideology.

So, quite apart from the ethical dilemmas involved in its use, science can never be totally value-neutral in its intellectual consequences. Within their models and metaphors, theories carry value-overtones. They violate Kant's prescriptions for the pure reason, in that they are never just neutral expressions of truth about nature, but always contain elements of practical judgement.

The mechanistic model has now been wholly discredited in science, and replaced by far more complex theories of holistic physical fields and undetermined futures, and by non-physically reducible models of life and mind. These are the new metaphors of science, which can become 'myths' if presented publicly as definitive answers to metaphysical and moral questions. Examples are computer-based models of mind which Fraser Watts and Eugene d'Aquili have discussed in their chapters. But the correct religious response to these new myths is not, I believe, to treat them as potential opponents of religion in their own terms, for example to announce that the mind and/or soul are nothing but organic information-systems. We should rather recognize that such metaphysical interpretations share some of the mythical functions of religion, and have to be judged accordingly. There are good and bad myths, and the decisions between them must depend on grounds of value and meaning which are out of reach of science itself.

Religion and Social Values

Which brings us to what sort of grounds these may be. It is easier to answer the question as to why we need religions, than to describe the criteria for judging between them, let alone determining their truth. Looking at the functions that have traditionally been performed by religion, it is clear that the need for a value-based social framework has not gone away, and is not provided by any surrogate from science, nor even by individualistic spiritualities or an innate moral sense. We live in social groups, not as isolated spiritual atoms, and cannot pick and choose according to individual whim among the many ways of life exhibited on the world scene. I see no evidence either that value-systems are ultimately viable when detached from some kind of metaphysical belief about human nature and the world, which religions and ideologies in general have always provided.

I believe we shall not understand the nature of religion, nor its comparative eclipse in the modern world, without facing these issues. They are not just philosophical and political issues, but also observable features of social life which call for attention in the studies that we call the 'human sciences'. There has been much discussion within the philosophy of science about whether the human sciences share exactly the same methodology and goals as the natural sciences. I cannot go into these disputes now, except to say that the general consensus is that their human subject-matter makes these sciences irreducibly different from the sciences of the natural world, and implies that methods and aims cannot entirely be shared. Partly for this reason, the sociological study of religion can act as a bridge between what I hope we can now perceive as the very different enterprises of natural science and religion.

Indeed religion itself has become a subject of sociological study. I have given examples from the natural sciences of attempts to find surrogates for God, but there is also at least one significant example from sociology of religion which is currently less discussed but may be somewhat more helpful. That is the pioneering study called *The Elementary Forms of the Religious Life* published in 1915 by Emile Durkheim.

Durkheim has sometimes been called the 'Father of Sociology', partly because of his empirical researches and philosophical discussion of *The Rules of Sociological Method*. But he also developed a profound philosophical thesis which he understood as a socialization of Kant's theory of knowledge. Where Kant looked for the innate necessities of the individual human mind in both the pure and the practical reason, Durkheim looked for the foundations of knowledge in the intrinsic workings of society. Indeed science itself may be studied as a social as well as a rational phenomenon. This approach has subsequently been pursued by many historians of science, and has contributed to a salutary placing of science as just one institution among others, with its distinctive features, but also with all the complex power and authority relations that its social nature implies.

Durkheim turned his attention particularly to religion as a social phenomenon, using the comparatively new late-nineteenth-century studies of exotic societies, including the indigenous Australians. He identified religion as that concerned with the sacred – things set apart, which yield symbolizations of the sacred by profane objects which thereby acquire power to structure and unify communities. Thus arise permissions and prohibitions in behaviour towards individuals, and between individuals and nature, which act as external constraints upon belief and practice, just as do natural facts. Durkheim argues that there must be some source outside the individual for the strength that such constraints have, but he declines to find this source in any reality transcending the empirical world. It is rather to be found in society itself, which is felt in primitive religions as a reality barely separable from nature. Society is God, the only surrogate for religion which we know to exist, but which is not reducible to either non-human nature nor to the individual human being. Religion therefore has its own autonomous existence as the space of sacred symbols, including of course sacred language and sacred ritual. In particular it underpins the ethical structure of a society, for which it provides symbolic social sanctions and psychological motivation.

Religion and Reality

This model has the merit of emancipating religion from individual subjectivism, and also from a pantheistic identity of God with aspects of the natural world. In these respects it is nearer than the natural scientific models to an adequate account of the actual phenomena of the world religions. But the stumbling block for traditional religious believers remains the transcendent reference of most religions, which Durkheim rejects. What is the status of the 'kingdom of ends' that is pointed to by Kant's *'What can we hope for?'*. After taking full account of the need for moral imperatives in a social context, we come back to the need for their metaphysical underpinning. I have rejected the claims of natural science to yield metaphysical truths that are relevant to religion, but even so we may find some useful parallels between the workings of metaphysical models in both types of discourse. Scientific models are analogous, not identical, with the observable world, but they cannot claim to capture the essence of 'reality'. This does not imply, however, that we are forbidden from speaking of a natural reality, whose essence we do not know, but which constrains the outcomes of experiments and the modest local theories we use to represent them. The ontological belief that there is a constraining reality, and that we can refer to it in the metaphorical language of models, does not depend on being able to represent it accurately, as is shown by the relative predictive success of past scientific theories that have subsequently been discarded as in principle false.

This is not linguistically very different from the way religious models refer to the realities that they claim exist. Models of God do not describe his essence, and are subject to radical changes from place to place and in the course of religious history. They relate to some things that are observable: to religious formalities, institutions and experiences, to social value-systems and conditions of cohesion and survival. These act in any given community as constraints upon the adequacy of its religious models. In terms of their social effects there are good and bad models in religion as in science.

To leave it at that would be the equivalent of simple instrumentalism in science, and would neglect the metaphysical questions. Belief in God implies his existence, but the relation between the existence of God and social and individual religious experience cannot be exactly the same as that between, for example, physical experiments and the reality of atoms, because we cannot have merely empirical criteria for a religion. Religion involves metaphysics and value-systems as well as 'facts'. Most attempts to overcome relativism at this level come to grief precisely on this methodological difference between empirical science and religion.

But perhaps we are mistaken in thinking that we can live without a pervasive abstract possibility of relativism. I call it 'abstract', because for most people for most of the time the individual choices of a way of life are severely limited. In most periods of history, indeed, the limits on choice have been total. It just has not been practically or, more important, imaginatively possible to step outside the social mores into which one was born. Our own society is indeed highly fragmented, but we are still essentially social animals. Perhaps we can do worse than consider again the rational bases of our own religious traditions, in the widest sense of Kant's 'rationalities'. In Christian as well as the related monotheisms of Judaism and Islam, there are far deeper insights and resources for social and individual life than are imagined in any sort of scientific humanism or Enlightenment rationalism. These insights can be made the starting-points of an understanding of the significance of both science and religion, not rejected as problematic archaisms which science has superseded.

Let me summarize in brief the answers I have tried to give to the original question 'Is Science the New Religion?' It was perhaps always a question expecting the answer 'No', but to spell out the reasons may have thrown some light on both science and religion. Science is not any sort of religion because:

1 It does not have any rational authority to put forward metaphysical claims about the origin, destiny, purpose or meaning of the universe. Its rational authority rests only on its successful organization and prediction of empirical data in comparatively local spatio-temporal regions, and on its consequent technological power.

2 When its models and metaphors are taken to be metaphysical truths, they become myths, to be judged on the same grounds as any other religious and ideological myths, against criteria which are not those of natural science.

3 These criteria include value-judgements about the pictures of the world and the human which scientific models put forth. At this level science itself is not value-neutral, and has often led to a general de-humanization of the world, a naïve view of the essential goodness of human nature, and a devaluation of the significance of society and human history.

4 Traditional religions have provided frameworks for these metaphysical and moral issues. They have consequent social functions which are needed but largely neglected in modern societies, because of a general scepticism about any rational authority other than science.

5 A restoration of the functions of religion will require attention to questions of meaning and value. Since these transcend empirical experience and literal language, there will have to be a revival of metaphorical language and mythological narrative within which to express them.

6 Since all these issues concern social life, which is largely pre-given to every individual in a society, we cannot patch up a religious framework *de novo*, but would do better to take our own religious traditions with renewed seriousness. Marrying Durkheim and Kant, this becomes the task of paying attention to what we should do, and what we can hope for, not in terms of Kant's innate and necessary principles, but in terms of the intimations of the 'sacred' which we have in our own traditions. This is a task which has to carry with it the conscious possibility of social relativism, and therefore a measure of tolerance. All the same it promises much more understanding than the essentially meaningless creed of a scientific humanist, which in its ultimate lack of anything realistic to hope for is perhaps more like stoicism than any other ideology in history.

Chapter Nine

THE GOD WHO IS WITH THE WORLD

Daniel W. Hardy

The Placing of the Question

Most of us will view the question of God and God's relation to the world through lenses formed by modern suppositions, which – as is growingly evident – are problematic in various ways. One major factor permeating our suppositions is the normalcy of distinctions: a series of distinctions have been made between various aspects of the world, and between these and God, and theories and applications have been developed for all of them independently. The result has been a fractured view of reality which continues to grow in its fragmentation. And – for a variety of reasons – some questions, particularly those which have to do with goodness and achieving it in this world, are rarely even asked.

Questions of the world, God and God's relation to the world, both those of their being and those of their goodness – are better posed within the more ancient view that they have to do with *wisdom*, which places them quite differently, as co-ordinated insights into reality. In fact, we need to resurrect the classical ideal 'of a single *sapientia* which holds within itself "the knowledge of all things human and divine" [Cicero] and knows how to express them with all the persuasive powers of *eloquentia*'.[1] But such a wisdom needs to be found within the possibilities of the world and God as we know them now, and therefore to be a modern wisdom.

Let us be clear about what this involves. Despite the modern bias to see everything as the product of human, and one's own, construction, wisdom designates more than the wisdom of human beings. It is the domain in which the dynamics of fundamental dimensions of the world and God are placed relative to each other, the domain – as you might call it – of relativities. Wisdom is therefore the *configuration* of insight – both theoretical and practical – into the multi-dimensionality of the world and God, not only how they are related but how they should be related. Correspondingly, it constitutes and constrains the ways in which the disciplined efforts of human beings to know and live with each other, the world and God are best deployed and shaped. Anyone who tries to understand how the world and God are related, and therefore how they are best approached, or how the various disciplines of human understanding are best related to each other, is involved in the search for, and finding of, wisdom – either directly or indirectly.

It is as much a matter of life as of understanding. Wisdom has also to do with the dynamic interwovenness, or interaction, of the world and humanity and God with each other, and how this is responsibly lived by those who are within it, not only as a matter of knowledge or understanding but as one of moral practice. How is responsibility for such an interwoven world assigned and distributed, and how is it met? How, furthermore, do these involve responsibility to God, and also godliness? In other words, lived wisdom is the dynamic of human knowledge, understanding and practice on the one hand, and God and the fulfilment of God's purposes on the other. The issue of wisdom is profoundly important for the relation of human knowledge, understanding and practice to God and God's purposes.

Wisdom is both within and beyond the scope of human understanding. Comprehending it is possible, and something we do unacknowledged at every moment, but it also far exceeds us. As the Book of Ecclesiasticus says, 'The first human never finished comprehending wisdom, nor will the last succeed in fathoming her.'[2] For special reasons, it may be necessary to emphasize the insufficiency of 'earthly wisdom', in order either to identify the distortions which it contains or to show the importance of God's grace. In the Epistle of James, it is said: 'This wisdom is not such as comes down from above, but is earthly, unspiritual, devilish' (James 3.15). Or Paul says: 'For our boast is this, the testimony of our conscience that we have behaved in the world, and still more toward you, with holiness and godly sincerity, not by earthly wisdom but by the grace of God' (2 Corinthians 1.12). Even in such cases, the grasp of wisdom is not denied. What is denied is the quality and sufficiency of particular kinds of comprehension, by reference to the dynamic of the work of God.

Wisdom in the positive sense designates not only the fundamental ordering of reality, its truth, but the rightness of this ordering, its goodness. Hence, wisdom is where the truth of reality coincides with its goodness; and this is necessarily eschatological. In the words of Lady Julian of Norwich, it is where

> All shall be well,
> and all shall be well,
> and all manner of thing shall be well.

Hence, it is where the aspects of reality in their truth and goodness, converge not abstractly or through abstract connections, but concretely.

For this reason, it has to do with fundamental 'relativities', how being and goodness are relative to each other and to God, and what is the dynamic of God's being and goodness in the real world. The purpose of the pursuit of wisdom is to uncover how things are ordered in relation to each other, not simply in their existence but in their fullness, as God is ordered in his fullness. It is a world-, self- and God-involving pursuit, through which one finds oneself – in every sense – in the dynamic of life. This is admirably put in this poem by the Irish poet Micheal O'Siadhail:

> A few are sitting this one out: spectators.
> Thinkers on the outside, catching a glance
> Of how the dancers turn like Plato's stars.
>
> Dance in a cosmos, cosmos in the light of dance.
> An ancient image, I know, stuff of visionaries:
> Harmony, music of spheres, the mystic's trance.
>
> The whirl of it! Barefaced and fluid boundaries,
> I'm watching through a window, sipping iced beer
> In the night air. Ripe images. Old quandaries.
>
> To dance between infinites of quark and star,
> Lost in a labyrinth we ourselves have planned.
> Detached and involved. Half-god, half-creature.
>
> Glimpse from a stillness beyond rhythm's command.
> An inner stillness in the shifting views of dancers.
> To stand under heavens you can never understand.[3]

It might be possible to watch and think of the related multi-dimensional dynamics of the world, humanity and God from a position 'on the outside', but we ourselves are actually both 'detached and involved', 'lost in a labyrinth we ourselves have planned'. And we are still within the dynamics of it all when we glimpse the 'inner stillness' of it all – something like what we call 'the peace of God which passes all understanding'. That is the world-, self-, other- and God-involving character of wisdom, highly dynamic yet at peace.

As I suggested at the outset, most of us view the question of God and God's relation to the world through lenses formed by modern suppositions, which cut apart these mutually involving elements and their dynamics. If the sciences and theology both had their place within wisdom, within the configuration of the dynamics of fundamental dimensions of the world and God relative to each other, they are more problematic now. We must pause to see how. Here is where we meet the limitations which have been placed upon the two on their way to the present.

Limitation 1: Wisdom as Knowledge

One limitation is found in the long-standing tradition of the West to translate wisdom into knowledge. In the case of someone such as St Thomas Aquinas, the wisdom of God – the source of all proper wisdom – is shared through the science of God whose subject-matter is revelation accessed through faith; and 'diverse natural sciences' were subordinated to this:

> The teaching of God is a single unified science. Whatever we know through scripture we know in one and the same way, by divine revelation; and there is one main subject-matter, with everything else treated as beginning or ending in God. As revealed by God, matter that would otherwise be the subject of diverse natural sciences, belongs to the one teaching, a sort of imprint of God's own knowledge in which everything is seen at once. For God in knowing himself knows all that he has made, so that his teaching transcends the distinction between pure and applied knowledge ...

> Doubts about the articles of faith [on which this teaching is based] arise not from any uncertainty in their subject-matter but from our feebleness in understanding. And that is why God's teaching sometimes makes use of other sciences, not as

superior sources of knowledge, but as subordinate ones with which human reason is more at home and from which it can more easily be led towards what transcends reason. This science shares in the wisdom of God, though it is not the wisdom we call a gift of the Holy Spirit.[4]

One problem with this is that it subordinates the good to what is known: 'Will seeks what the mind presents as good, so God can only will what his wisdom, as a sort of just law, decrees to be right.'[5] Where this strategy is followed, wisdom as the correlative understanding and performance of the world, goodness and God becomes something much thinner, the knowing of what is to be known, from revelation or the world or a combination of the two.

What this did was to sunder truth from goodness, equating goodness with a truthful theory and disconnecting it from practice. An insight into the problem which this generated is found in the agony which Martin Luther suffered over the interpretation of Chapter 1 of Paul's Epistle to the Romans, and how – in his famous 'breakthrough' – he was transformed:

> Hitherto I had been held up – not by a 'lack of heat in my heart's blood', but by one word only, in chapter 1: 'The righteousness [*iustitia*] of God is revealed in [the Gospel].' For I hated this word 'righteousness of God', which by the customary use of all the doctors I had been taught to understand philosophically as what they call the *formal* or *active righteousness* whereby God is just and punishes unjust sinners.
>
> For my case was this: however irreproachable my life as a monk, I felt myself in the presence of God [*coram Deo*] to be a sinner with a most unquiet conscience, nor could I believe him to be appeased by the satisfaction I could offer. I did not love – nay I hated this just God who punishes sinners . . .
>
> At last, as I meditated day and night, God showed mercy and I turned my attention to the connection of the words, namely – 'The righteousness of God is revealed, as it is written: the righteous shall live by faith' – and there I began to understand that the righteousness of God is the righteousness in which a just man lives by the gift of God, in other words by faith . . . At this I felt myself straightway born afresh and to have entered through the open gates into paradise itself.[6]

Luther's dilemma was to be caught in a *knowledge* of accepted principles which was incapable of restoring a troubled sinner; it simply did not connect with his *moral* dis-ease, his 'unquiet conscience'. It was only when he discovered that the goodness (justice) of God was present, not as scientific knowledge but as the working of God in life itself – the goodness of God transforming life to goodness – that he found the full meaning of goodness. Afterward, however, while in practice he held truth and goodness in tension, Luther did not succeed in restoring the interpenetration of truth and goodness which is characteristic of wisdom. The problem of the severance of the two, and the subordination of the latter to the former, remained.

Limitation 2: The Severance of Wisdom (Knowledge)
from Its Source

A second limitation imposed on the notion of wisdom was to suppose that it was only invisible and unchangeable. As Augustine said,

> This divine Wisdom is not only invisible, ... but unchangeable ... This unchangeableness of Wisdom is rehearsed by the text, *Abiding in herself she renews all things* (Wis 7:27) ... the substance of the one and only God, that is of the Father and of the Son and of the Holy Spirit, remains not only invisible but also unchangeable, and therefore abides in true and genuine immortality. As for us, we say that God has never shown himself to bodily eyes, neither the Father nor the Son nor the Holy Spirit, except through some created bodily substance at the service of his power.[7]

This view of the invisibility and unchangeability of Wisdom in God, accessible only through 'some created bodily substance at the service of his power', was shared by Aquinas and Luther, not to mention Calvin.

The Wisdom of God was only accessible – and then as knowledge – in revelation received in faith. Luther and Calvin invoked the Wisdom of God as a transcendental contradiction to worldly wisdom; and they concluded that this Wisdom of God is accessible only in a radical faith, while Aquinas located wisdom in first principles which are beyond the problems of the world. Luther's and Calvin's response was resolutely theocentric and Christic, where the medieval one was metaphysical.

But in all cases, a disjunction occurred between the source of true knowledge (and practice) and worldly wisdom.

Perhaps you know the story told about a US farmer in Maine, a largely rural state 100 miles or so north east of the city of Boston. One evening, he was rocking on the porch of his house when a rather flashy car drove up, the window slid down and the driver shouted, 'How do you get to Boston from here?' The farmer replied, 'Go straight down the road, turn right at the fork, then left at the . . . No, you can't do it that way.' Then he paused, thought a little, and said, 'Turn your car around, and go back to the crossing a mile back, turn left, then right at the . . . No, you can't go there that way.' He paused again, thought some more, and tried again, only to stop again. Finally, after rocking and thinking for some time, with the traveller growing visibly more impatient, he said, 'Sorry, mister, you can't get there from here.' That is the kind of limitation placed on wisdom rooted solely in this world.

Where Aquinas, and Calvin also, incorporated such attempts within 'scientific knowledge' of God as legitimate uses of reason which implied what transcends reason, in due course such limitations became unacceptable to the emerging forms of knowledge. The disjunction of knowledge from a transcendent source and goal, and making knowledge instrumental to this transcendent source, were resisted by those who developed modern scientific practices.

Even more strikingly, the very possibility that there was an eternally unchanging Wisdom from which all knowledge derived seemed to be at odds with the ordering of the dimensions of the world which preoccupied modern minds. Indeed, such a Wisdom disappeared 'behind' the spatial dimensionality and the temporal changeability of the world, except of course for those prepared to subscribe to the fairly rigid patterns in which the world, humanity and God were said to be known through faith.

The fragments of wisdom which now emerged from the cognitive searchings of modern scientific attempts were *knowledge*, however. And as such there was minimal reference to the dynamics of the truth and goodness of the multi-dimensional world from and to God which had been the concerns of the old wisdom. And this in turn produced an inability to deal with the moral implications of the knowledge which was achieved, and a blindness to consequences. It was legitimate to seek knowledge for its own sake.

Progressively, furthermore, whether in the sciences or in theology, these attempts followed more and more narrow paths, which divided them from each other and further fragmented the possibility of wisdom. This is easily seen in the patterns of academic study which emerged in universities. These patterns achieved their present form in the late nineteenth century: academic institutions were organized in departments, where academic professionals were to train the professional élites needed in the wider society; now, even in departments or faculties, there is further division, as professionals follow the norms of particular specialist fields.

Hence, the various disciplines dedicated to demarcated dimensions of the world have sought to produce 'universal' conclusions. And in fact they have produced firm conclusions which are used to justify the purity of the disciplines themselves – creation without a Creator, evolution without a designer, culture without the Word of God, religions which are incommensurable, God known only through cognition in faith, and so forth. All this overlooks the interpenetration of the dimensions of the world which is characteristic of wisdom. Actually, the dimensions of the world are not so neatly demarcated as such organization of learning suggests; there is – as one might say – an 'ooziness' in wisdom. This would lead us to expect these dimensions, and the disciplines dedicated to them, to recognize each other as important. Although this happens more often than people admit, purists tend to overlook or even despise it.[8]

So, as we see, wisdom severed from its source in the Wisdom of God, and pursued as specialized forms of knowledge, loses its unity and its concern for goodness. By now we assume that this fragmentation and dissociation from goodness is normal.

Wisdom and the Task of Theology

If wisdom is understanding and living the dynamics of the fundamental dimensions of the world and God relative to each other, the main problems stem from the distortions introduced by the suppositions we have just reviewed. We must learn to move beyond them, by reopening the possibility of wisdom as the meaning of the world which is immersed in its very being (not abstract from it), a meaning in which divine meaning is present, where God – by virtue of God's meaning – is active in the very constitution of the meaning of the world.

It is a multifold task, requiring us freshly to recognize the multi-dimensional dynamics of the world in which we are involved, to appreciate and follow their trajectory and to uncover the activity of God in them. The different aspects of that task are often neglected, because those responsible pursue very restricted forms of knowledge, avoid the full scope of issues and relevant disciplines and evade the primary focus, God. The task of theology within wisdom will be to locate the basis in God's life and action for the constituting factors of human life in this world – for the dynamic multi-dimensionality of the world. Hence the title of this chapter, 'The God Who Is With the World'.

It is important to recognize that this multifold task does not impose an unusual requirement either on the sciences or on theology. A look at the history of the intersection of the various attempts to understand and live the dynamics of the fundamental dimensions of the world, and their interaction with theology, suggests that human understanding of these issues advances correlatively. The understanding of the world has been tested and enlarged by attempts to think and live responsibly in the world from and with and to God, and vice versa. Worldly knowledge and practice have sought freedom from the attempt of theology to instrumentalize them; and the understanding of God has suffered proportionately from reactive attempts to safeguard theology. There have been 'extreme[s] of exaggerated expectations of innerworldly fulfillment and transformation',[9] and theology has been locked into the position of a self-sustaining form of knowledge in reaction to them. Nevertheless, it remains the case that each has normally been made more profound and worthwhile through engagement with the other, other ways of considering the world interacting with the attempt to understand God and God's work (theology).

The Reopening of Wisdom

Perhaps the most significant way by which to reopen wisdom, as the finding of the meaning of the multi-dimensional world in which we are involved as one in which divine meaning, the activity of God, is present, is through worship. For worship is the situation in which people seek explicitly and wholly to participate in the dynamic of the world as conditioned by its most fundamental constitutive source. In that sense, even the sciences are vestigially worship.

It is in worship where the most profound issues appear, what is and should be the case in the world, and how being itself and life are – and are to be – shaped within the dynamic conditioned by God. Attending to these issues requires intimacy with them, involvement with the world and with God in ways appropriate to them. Ultimately, worship is called forth from us by the sufficiency of the One who constitutes the dynamic order of the world.

One gets a sense of that range of involvements in this quotation from an American Indian:

> I was born in Nature's wide domain! The trees were all that sheltered my infant limbs, the blue heavens all that covered me. I am one of Nature's children. I have always admired her. She shall be my glory: her features, her robes, and the wreath about her brow, the seasons, her stately oaks, and the evergreen – her hair, ringlets over the earth – all contribute to my enduring love of her.

> And wherever I see her, emotions of pleasure roll in my breast, and swell and burst like waves on the shores of the ocean, in prayer and praise to Him who has placed me in her hand.[10]

In this, there is an intimate connection between the meaning found in the life of the world – its fundamental truth, goodness and beauty – and the One through whom this human being is placed within it. In this case, worship is the assigning of worth to that One who has so made the conditions of the world as to place this human being in it. This worship begins and remains in the dynamics of the multi-dimensional world, and out of the order and goodness found there praises the One who has made and makes it thus – ordered in its goodness, and good in its orderliness. To do such a thing is to gather the complex nature and goodness of the world into the act of giving honour to the One who so constituted it.

Such worship is the reopening of wisdom – by which the dynamics of the world are constituted – to its constituting source, thereby recovering the ultimate nature and goodness of its origin. As such it operates within the world to relate it to the source of its order, goodness and life, in order to remind us how to relive that within the less-than-pristine circumstances of the world as it is.

Amidst the meaning found in the world, worship is where there is a focusing on the One in whom this order, goodness and life are fully realized, in whom the honour attributed in worship is therefore inherent or immanent. Hence, in such worship, supremely positive value is found to be inherent in one God who infinitely transcends – not spatially but qualitatively – lesser forms of unity, truth, goodness and beauty whether visible or not, in such a way that there is no basis of comparison between this God and them. It is because the meaning found in the world is found to be *from* One in whom meaning is fully realized that the appropriate expression of worship is the finding and expressing of the honour and glory that is *in* the God in whom there is all worth, not on honour given by human beings. Hence honour or glory is God's, and only derivatively in the gift of one who does honour to God.

What is found is that God – as the ultimately defining reality – is the source by which the configurations of the dynamics of the multi-dimensional world are constituted, both in their nature and in their goodness. It is not that the particular characteristics of the world – those on which so much attention has been lavished by those who wish to ascertain their order through the search for the 'laws' which govern them – are unimportant, but that they are here seen in their placing in the dynamics of the world itself. And the same can be said of God: it is not that the search for the particular character of God – what is the consistency of God's freedom by which God is God – is unimportant, but that here it is seen in the dynamics of God's activity in the multi-dimensional world, in its meaning for the world.

And the particularities of things found in the world – as differentiated from each other and from God – are found to be those which are established by God, and the nature of their independence established by God, although the ways in which they are particular are always those of the multi-dimensional world. For example, 'the world' is constituted as distinct, but even this distinctness is one maintained as the expression of God's positive valuation. If, however, particularities in the world take possession of their distinctiveness as 'themselves', a possibility which inheres in them by virtue of the fact that they are given genuine distinctness by God, they will be at odds with the true character of their distinctness.

The same applies to the distinctions which are brought about in creation by God. In the understanding of worship which we have been tracing, the existence and nature of the otherness of things from each other is found to be constituted by God, and they are thereby proportioned to achieve their fullest, while not overreaching themselves. In their valuation by God, they are neither alien from each other, nor in relations of domination one to another. If they constitute and develop their own otherness from each other in such a way as to alienate and dominate each other, they misconstrue their relations and thus contradict the source and nature of their distinctness.

There is an important issue here. We have been suggesting that wisdom – as the configuration of the dynamics of fundamental dimensions of the world and God relative to each other – is actually reopened in worship. And if these dynamics include the otherness of things from each other and from God, and relations between them which are proportioned in such a way as to enable them to achieve their fullness, what kind of God is found in worship?

What Kind of God is Found in Worship?

We need to distinguish two inadequate answers before looking at a more adequate one.

The most problematic answer to this question correlates two forms of dynamics, one consisting of quasi-mechanical forms of interaction between things in the world (including human beings) and the other a quasi-mechanical order from which these are thought to be derived. That is the issue recognized by Steven Weinberg:

> It seems to me that if the word 'God' is to be of any use, it should be taken to mean an interested God, a creator and lawgiver who has established not only the laws of nature and the universe but also standards of good and evil, some personality that is concerned with our actions, something in short that it is appropriate for us to worship. This is the God that has mattered to men and women throughout history. Scientists and others sometimes use the word 'God' to mean something so abstract and unengaged that He is hardly likely to be distinguished from the laws of nature. Einstein once said that he believed in 'Spinoza's God who reveals Himself in the orderly harmony of what exists, not in a God who

concerns himself with fates and actions of human beings'. But what possible difference does it make to anyone if we use the word 'God' in place of 'order' or 'harmony,' except perhaps to avoid the accusation of having no God? . . . it seems to me that it makes the concept of God not so much wrong as unimportant.[11]

In such a case, as Weinberg sees, one form of wisdom traced to God – nature measured by 'standards of good and evil' traced to an 'interested God' interested in our actions – has been supplanted by another – laws of nature traced to 'immanent order' grandiosely called 'God'. The laws of nature traced to an 'unimportant' notion of God are not the 'nature' and 'God' which we find in worship, for two reasons: the dynamics of nature are restricted to 'laws', with no reference to goodness; and the possibility of a God from whose good being the constraints of the world are constituted, is excluded.

What is often provided as a contradiction to this 'unimportant' God is a view of God as the fundamental determinant of the particularities and dynamics of the world, as the meaning within which all other meaning is subsumed. The view which we saw earlier – that the Wisdom which orders the world derives solely from God by means of revelation – can yield a rigid dogmatic system which is profoundly problematic both for the multi-dimensional dynamics of the world and for the God by whose activity they are constituted and sustained.

How? As we saw, worship reopens the dynamics of fundamental dimensions of the world and God relative to each other – those dynamics which are wisdom. Such dynamics will include the world and humanity in all their aspects, as from and to the dynamics of the being and goodness of God. But this can be narrowed into a rigid dogmatic system which, while claiming derivation from the revelation of God, actually confines within its specifications (1) the God who is known, (2) how to know and (3) the possibilities for knowledge, limiting all of these to what the system will allow. The technique reminds me of what is often done by people who cannot cope with the complex tasks which confront them: they narrow the tasks to those they can deal with. This is tunnel vision, through which the object, and the methods and scope of knowing, are restricted. The very 'certitude' which it provides can then authorize attempts to refine the object and methods, mistaking the credibility of the details provided, while at the same time disallowing the legitimacy of attending to other objects and methods – and even oppressing those who would, in the name of God, be concerned with them.

It is important to move beyond both these strategies, the 'unimportant' God and a 'narrowly important' God, to one which does indeed reopen the dynamics of fundamental dimensions of the world and God relative to each other. The way forward seems to be to recognize and live in the mutual participation of these dynamics, while tracing this participation to God. That is exactly what happens in worship. In the words of Alan Torrance:

> Christian worship becomes thus the free participation by the Spirit in something that God perfects on our behalf . . . Christian worship shares in a human–Godward movement that belongs to God and which takes place *within* the divine life. It is precisely into and within *this* that we are brought by the Spirit to participate as a gift of grace . . . Worship is not some valiant subjective response, therefore. It is a gift of grace which is realised vicariously in Christ and which is received and participated in by the Spirit. It speaks of a *theosis* or *theopoiesis* whose form and content are 'from above'.[12]

Hence, the very reopening of oneself to participation in the dynamics of the world which occurs in worship is one by which we participate in 'a human–Godward movement that belongs to God and which takes place *within* the divine life'. And we should remind ourselves that such participation in the dynamics of the world as from the movement of the divine meaning in us is not simply a cognitive one whereby we trace the conditions of doing so. It is participation in order to effect the goodness which derives from such mutual participation.

The God (who is) with the World

Such understanding incorporates a very rich set of conceptions about the nature of God and God's active relations with the world, which for Christians is spelled out in terms of the Trinity and the economy of divine action in the history of the world. Instead of a God who has disappeared into the order of the world (the 'unimportant God' discussed earlier), and in place of a God whose being and action are confined within a rigid dogmatic system (the 'narrowly important God'), it is closer to the fullness of God to work in the varieties of ways which are appropriate to the multi-dimensional dynamics of the world to achieve its proper constitution and goodness. And these are more likely to be innerworldly ones interwoven with different and multiple kinds of agency from and to God, the effect being to fill them with the richness which is characteristic of God's own life. That is ultimately the best argument for the Trinitarian character of God.

The correlative understanding of nature is less simple and closed than those which suppose the primacy of self-contained natural processes. It supposes a view of nature as open and contingent, in which natural agents are less closely structured and are capable of exercising such responsibility as is theirs to perform, but do so by being raised up to their eventual purpose. In such a world, entities have contingent structure and interrelations through the exercise of their self-constitutive power in their relations. And the effect of the work of God is in their interactive self-constitution, through which they are raised to what they may become. While it remains possible for human beings to suppose that the world is comprised of closed systems of linear causality, whether within the natural world or in their relations to God, such systems are in fact the idealizations of limited aspects of what – seen more fully – is a nature which is open, contingent and awaiting its fulfilment. Such a situation is richly indicated in another poem by Micheal O'Siadhail:

> Like pegs, our forearms held the skein's coil.
> Arcs of the knitter's hand unloop
> and ball by turn. Sweep and detail.
> A feeling of beginning in childhood's wind-up
> I keep on recalling. Somehow I'm between
> a yarn uncoiling to a tight ball of destiny,
> a ball unravelling back the promise of a skein.
> Plain stitch and design; point and infinity.
> Who changes the world? Oh, this and that,
> strands as they happen to fall, tiny ligatures,
> particular here and nows, vast loopings
> of pattern, the ties and let-gos of a knot,
> small X-shapes of history; our spoor and signature
> a gauze of junctures, a nettedness of things.
>
> Whose music? A quiver enters like a spirit,
> a murmur of tension from and back

into space. A tune of trembles in catgut.
The pride of an instrument as at its beck
and call the heart vibrates: pulse-sway,
dominion of rhythm, power before the slack
and silence. 'Pride before a fall' we say,
sic transit . . . Should we've been puritans,
taut, untouchable, our unshakeable self-mastery
a vacuum of muteness? O noise of existence
shake in me a tone you need; sweet
friction of rosin, play me limp or tense.
Possessor of everything, owner of nothing
Whose bow shivers its music in my string?[13]

The poem makes clear the active bestowal by its source of the highly contingent complexity of all being and activity, in which are interwoven nature and God's action. It is that very contingency which opens freedom for each element of nature, while also providing the scope and parameters within which it may operate. At the same time, this freedom is constituted and activated (energized) by the free ordering of God, by which it is blessed and enriched.

It seems, therefore, the relatedness of God to the fabric of nature is far more complex than is generally thought. God's ongoingly active and energetic self-structuring in the bestowal and sustenance of the highly contingent complexity in which being-in-relation consists, provides a far more complex and contingent relation between him and innerworldly being. That is not to say that the marks of God's presence in this cannot be found, pre-eminently in the ordered energy which activates it to realize itself in relation to God. The highest sign of the blessing which God confers is in the blessing which each entity brings to others, and thereby to him.

It is the task of Christian theology to discern the Trinitarian God who is himself by the economy of his presence in the world. This God maintains the consistency of his life in an ordered but energetic congruence with his world, through self-restructuring in a free, coherent and abundant response to the perturbations (constructive or destructive) which occur in that interaction and in those with whom he interacts.

What is God actually like – the God who is thus active in the world? God's own unity is what can be called the 'coherence of abundance', energetic in self-conferral in love and hope, and therefore self-constituting in God's gift of himself. As thus seen, the Triune God is an energetic (Spirit-driven) unity in God which arises from the unfathomable abundance of love and hope which is primary to God (what we designate by the word 'Father') and which becomes 'operative' through God's interaction with the contingencies of life and death in the world (that is, in 'the Son'). Correspondingly, the dynamics of the world – and even the circumstances of alienation, hostility and incomprehension into which these dynamics have 'fallen' – become the means through which this God manifests the truth and goodness of his wisdom.

But this is not so much an explanation of a 'state of affairs' in God as it is an account of the energetically consistent congruence with the world by which God follows his own unfathomable abundance of love and hope to the fulfilment of the existence and goodness of the world. In more formal terms, it is 'energetic' through the operation of the Holy Spirit, and 'coherent in its primary abundance' (of love and hope) through the Father's relation to the Son. The energy of this coherence of abundance makes the 'fierce and excited contingency' through which the Spirit 'excites' the fulfilment of the primary conditions of God – love and hope – in the world through God's congruence with the world in an ongoing self-structuring of God and the world. It is this which makes God the dynamic structured relationality in whom there is the infinite possibility of truth, goodness and life for the world.

The activity of God in the multi-dimensional dynamics of the world is not through a simple agency, as if God simply 'did' or 'does' the world or things in it. Nor is it to be confined to one person of the Trinity, whether the power of the Father or the constituting and reconstituting presence of Christ, or the moving of the Holy Spirit. The activity of God in the interwovenness of the world is differentiated but 'all of a piece': the operation of the Holy Spirit achieves its consistency by following the primary conditions which we conventionally identify as the 'Father' and the congruence with the world which we identify as the 'Son'.

What occurs in the life of the Trinitarian God is an outpouring of energy through which the primary conditions of God are fulfilled, but through the congruence of God with the world. God is fulfilled in his constitution and active sustenance of the interwovenness of the world as it moves toward its fulfilment in goodness. Words for this fulfilment are difficult, but the language of 'blessing' and 'glorifying' may be best, for they signify the intensification of ordered life which occurs in God and from God in the interwovenness of the world for its well-being. So far as God himself is concerned, it is a concentration of energy in the very being of God, which is manifest in the fullness of God's work in the world.[14] The activity of this Triune God is the source of the dynamics of the world, as it is constituted and shaped for its future fulfilment. The activity of this God sustains a dynamic complexity of particularities, and moves within it to fulfil the world's goodness in himself.

Conclusion

By seeking for the wisdom by which to understand and live in the dynamics of a multi-dimensional world, and avoiding some of the limitations usually imposed on the task, we have found that worship – in which many aspects and tensions of the world are brought together – may reopen the possibility of a wisdom for the world in which God is active as source, sustenance, correction and fulfilment – to bring the world to its true being and goodness. As found in this worship, the Triune God who is with the world is by nature 'interested' in it and at work to restore it and bring it to its goodness.

NOTES

Chapter Two: Beyond the Big Bang

1 Hawking, S., *A Brief History of Time*. London, Bantam, 1988.
2 Tipler, F. J., *The Physics of Immortality*. Basingstoke, Macmillan, 1994.

Chapter Three: Uncertainties of Science

1 Peacocke, A. R., *Creation and the World of Science*. Oxford, Oxford University Press, 1979, p. 46.
2 Boyle, R., quoted in Westfall, R. S., *The Construction of Modern Science*. New York, Wiley and Sons, 1971; republished by Cambridge University Press, 1977, p. 115.
3 Newton, I., *Opticks*. 1704 Bk. I, Pt II, Prop X, Prob. V.
4 Cook, Alan, *The Observational Foundations of Physics*. Cambridge, Cambridge University Press, 1994.
5 Cook, *The Observational Foundations of Physics*.
6 Ferrière, R. and Fox, G. A., Chaos and evolution. *TREE* (Elsevier), 10, pp. 480–4, 1995.
7 Williams, B., *Shame and Necessity*. Oxford, University of California Press, 1993.
8 Polkinghorne, J., *Creatio continua* and divine action. *Science and Christian Belief* 7, pp. 101–8, 1995. Peacocke, A., A Response to Polkinghorne. *Science and Christian Belief* 7, pp. 109–115, 1995.
9 Ferrière, R. and Fox, G. A., Chaos and evolution. *TREE* 10, p. 484, 1995.

Chapter Four: Evolution and Creation

1 As reviewed by Hayes, J. M. in *Nature*, Vol. 384, p. 21, 7 November 1996.
2 See, for example, Blackmore, V. and Page, A., *Evolution – the Great Debate*. Oxford, Lion Publishing, 1989.
3 *Nature*, Vol. 171, p. 737.

4   As reviewed by Holder, N. and McMahon, A. in *Nature*, Vol. 383, p. 515, 12 December 1996.

5   Described by Nusse, R. in *Nature*, Vol. 384, 14 November 1996.

6   Morris, H. M., *King of Creation*. Christian Literature Press, San Diego, 1980.

7   *The Economist*, 17 August 1996.

8   Gish, D. T., A consistent biblical and scientific view of origins. In Burke, D. (ed.), *Creation and Evolution*. Leicester, Inter-Varsity Press, 1985, p. 191.

9   See Burke (ed.), *Creation and Evolution*, pp. 46 ff.

10 See Burke (ed.), *Creation and Evolution*, pp. 139 ff.

11 See Burke (ed.), *Creation and Evolution*, pp. 91 ff.

12 See Peacocke, A. R., *God and New Biology*. London, Dent, 1986; reprinted by Peter Smith, Gloucester, Mass.

13 Monod, J., *Chance and Necessity*. London, Collins, 1972.

14 Dawkins, R., *Climbing Mount Improbable*. London, Viking, 1996. (Reviewed by Kauffman, S. in *Nature*, Vol. 382, p.309, 25 July 1996.)

15 Reprinted from *Science and Christian Belief* 6(1), April 1994 and 7(1), April 1995.

16 Dawkins, R., *The Blind Watchmaker*. London, Longman, 1986.

17 See *Science and Christian Belief* 6(1), April 1994, p. 48.

18 For example Behe, M. J., *Darwin's Black Box: The Biochemical Challenge to Evolution*. New York, Free Press/Simon & Schuster, 1996.

19 In a personal communication.

Chapter Five: Brain, Mind and Soul

1   Midgley, M., *Science as Salvation: A Modern Myth and its Meaning*. London, Routledge, 1992.

2   Dennett, D. C., *Consciousness Explained*. Harmondsworth, Penguin, 1991, p. 21.

3   Flanagan, O., *Consciousness Reconsidered*. Cambridge, Mass., MIT Press, 1992, p. 222.

4   Craig, E., *The Mind of God and the Works of Man*. Oxford, Clarendon Press, 1987.

5   Crick, F., *The Astonishing Hypothesis: The Scientific Search for the Soul*. London, Simon & Schuster, 1994. For a critical review, see Watts, F., Are we really nothing more than our neurones? *Journal of Consciousness Studies* 1, pp. 275–9, 1994.

6   See Peacocke, A. R. (ed.), *Reductionism in Academic Disciplines*. Guildford, NFER, 1985.

7   See Jeeves, M. A., *Human Nature at the Millennium*. Grand Rapids, Baker Books, 1997.

8   On religious issues raised by AI, see Puddefoot, J., *God and the Mind Machine*. London, SPCK, 1996. On more general philosophical

issues, see Copeland, J., *Artificial Intelligence: A Philosophical Intro-duction.* Oxford, Blackwell, 1993.

9 For Watts, see *The Tablet,* 13 November 1993; for Furse see *The Tablet,* 20 November 1993.

10 Hillman, J., *Re-visioning Psychology.* New York, Harper & Row, 1975, p. x.

11 Ryle, G., *The Concept of Mind.* London, Hutchinson, 1949.

12 Ward, K., *Defending the Soul.* Oxford, One World, 1992.

13 Peacocke, A. R., *Theology for a Scientific Age.* London, SCM Press, 1993, chapter 11.

14 See Meissner, W. W., *Ignatius of Loyola: The Psychology of a Saint.* New Haven, Yale University Press, 1992.

15 See Proudfoot, W., *Religious Experience.* Berkeley, University of California Press, 1986. For a contrasting point of view, see Forman, R. K. C., Of capsules and carts: Mysticism, language, and the via negativa. *Journal of Consciousness Studies,* 1, pp. 38–49, 1994.

16 Barfield, O., *The Rediscovery of Meaning and Other Essays.* Middle-town, Conn., University Press of New England (Wesleyan University Press), 1977. Also Watts, F. and Williams, M., *The Psychology of Religious Knowing.* Cambridge, Cambridge University Press, 1988; reissued by Geoffrey Chapman, 1994, chapter 7.

Chapter Six: The Neuropsychology of Religion

1 Schleiermacher, F., *On Religion,* trans J. Oman. London, Kegan Paul, 1893.

2 Durkheim, E., *The Elementary Forms of the Religious Life.* New York, Macmillan, 1926.

3 Otto, R., *The Idea of the Holy.* New York, Oxford University Press, 1970; original German edition: *Das Heilige,* Marburg, 1917.

4 Eliade, M., *The Sacred and the Profane.* New York, Harcourt, Brace, and Jovanovich, 1959.

5 King, W., Religion. In Eliade, M. (ed.), *The Encyclopedia of Religion.* Vol. 12. New York, Macmillan, 1978, pp. 284–5.

6 King. In Eliade (ed.), *The Encyclopedia of Religion.* Vol. 12, p. 288.

7 d'Aquili, E. G., The neurological basis of myth and concepts of deity. *Zygon* 13, p. 257, 1978. d'Aquili, E. G., The myth-ritual com-plex: A biogenetic structural analysis. *Zygon* 18, pp. 247–69, 1983. d'Aquili, E. G., Myth, ritual, and the archetypal hypothesis: Does the dance generate the word? *Zygon* 21, pp. 141–60, 1986. d'Aquili, E. G. and Laughlin, C., The biopsychological determinants of religious ritual behaviour. *Zygon* 10, pp. 32–58, 1975.

8 The inferior parietal lobule on the dominant side, the anterior convexity of the frontal lobes primarily on the dominant side, and their reciprocal neural interconnections have been fairly defini-tively shown to account for causal sequencing of elements of reality

abstracted from sense perceptions. The operation of cross-modal transfer, which is particularly noted in the function of the inferior parietal lobule, is implicated in causal sequencing. The inferior parietal lobule roughly corresponds to areas of the brain located at the confluence of the parietal, occipital, and temporal lobes. For convenience we refer to the anterior convexity of the frontal lobe, the inferior parietal lobule and their reciprocal interconnections as the 'causal operator'.

9 Gimello, R., Mysticism and mediation. In Katz, S. (ed.), *Mysticism and Philosophical Analysis*. New York, Oxford University Press, 1978, p. 178.

10 Streng, F., Language and mystical awareness. In Katz (ed.), *Mysticism and Philosophical Analysis*.

11 Smart, N., *Reasons and Faiths: An Investigation of Religious Discourse, Christian and Non-Christian*. London, Routledge and Kegan Paul, 1958. Smart, N., History of mysticism. In Edwards, P. (ed.), *Encyclo-pedia of Philosophy*. London, Macmillan, 1967. Smart, N., *The Religious Experience of Mankind*. London, Macmillan, 1969. Smart, N., Understanding religious experience. In Katz (ed.), *Mysticism and Philosophical Analysis*.

12 Stace, W. T., *Mysticism and Philosophy*. London, Macmillan, 1961.

13 Katz, S., Language, epistemology, and mysticism. In Katz (ed.), *Mysticism and Philosophical Analysis*.

14 d'Aquili, E. G., Laughlin, C. and McManus, J., *The Spectrum of Ritual: A Biogenetic Structural Analysis*. New York, Columbia University Press, 1979. d'Aquili and Laughlin, The biopsychological determinants of religious ritual behaviour. d'Aquili, The myth-ritual complex: A biogenetic structural analysis. d'Aquili, E. G. and Newberg, A. B., Religious and mystical states: A neuropsychological substrate. *Zygon* 28, pp. 177–200, 1993. d'Aquili, E. G. and Newberg, A. B., Liminality, trance and unitary states in ritual and meditation. *Studia Liturgica* 23, pp. 2–34, 1993.

15 d'Aquili, The neurological basis of myth and concepts of deity.

16 d'Aquili and Laughlin, The biopsychological determinants of religious ritual behaviour. d'Aquili and Newberg, Religious and mystical states: A neuropsychological substrate. d'Aquili and Newberg, Liminality, trance and unitary states in ritual and meditation.

17 d'Aquili and Newberg, Religious and mystical states: A neuropsychological substrate. d'Aquili and Newberg, Liminality, trance and unitary states in ritual and meditation.

18 d'Aquili, Myth, ritual, and the archetypal hypothesis: Does the dance generate the word?

19 d'Aquili, Senses of reality in science and religion: A neuroepistemological perspective. *Zygon* 17, p. 361, 1982.

20 d'Aquili, Senses of reality in science and religion: A neuroepistemological perspective. d'Aquili and Newberg, Religious and

mystical states: A neuropsychological substrate. d'Aquili and Newberg, Liminality, trance and unitary states in ritual and meditation.

In all likelihood, the neurological substrate for the holistic operator involves the function of a part of the parietal lobe on the non-dominant side. We have presented a model which attempts to explain the attainment of Absolute Unitary Being by integrating Hess's ergotropic–trophotropic model with the split-brain research considered by other investigators. (See Bogen, J. E., The other side of the brain, II: An appositional mind. *Bulletin of Los Angeles Neurological Society* 34, pp. 135–62, 1969. Sperry, R. W., Lateral specialization in surgically separated hemispheres. In Vinken, P. J. and Bruyn G. W. (eds.), *The Neurosciences: Third Study Program*. Cambridge, Mass., MIT Press, 1974. Travarthen, C., Brain bisymmetry and the role of the corpus callosum in behaviour and conscious experience. Presented at the International Colloquium on Interhemispheric Relations, Czechoslovakia, June 10–13, 1969. In our model, we proposed that the ergotropic system actually extended upwards to include the dominant hemisphere and that the trophotropic system extended upwards to include the non-dominant hemisphere. By driving either one or the other system to a state of saturation we postulated that the opposite system would be briefly stimulated as we know occurs in third state autonomic stimulation such that, for a brief period, there would be firing of both systems.

21 Schwartz, G. E., Davidson, R. J., and Maer, F., Right hemisphere lateralization for emotion in the human brain: Interactions with cognitions. *Science* 190, pp. 286–8, 1975.

22 d'Aquili, Myth, ritual, and the archetypal hypothesis: Does the dance generate the word?

23 Schwartz, Davidson and Maer, Right hemisphere lateralization for emotion in the human brain: Interactions with cognitions.

Chapter Seven: Science and Religion: Contest or Confirmation?

1 Lady Strachey (ed.), *Letters of Edward Lear*, 1907.

2 Stoneley, R. in Mitchison, N. (ed.), *Outline for Boys and Girls and Their Parents*. London, Gollancz, 1932, p. 363.

3 de Riencourt, A., *The Eye of the Shiva: Eastern Mysticism and Science*. London, Souvenir, 1980, pp. 196f.

4 Lucretius, *de Rerum Natura* 1. 101, 183: 'How many evils has religion caused! . . . Religion has brought forth criminal and impious deeds.'

5 Butler, S., *Notebooks*, 1912.

6   See Bowker, J., *The Sense of God: Sociological, Anthropological and Psychological Approaches to the Origin of the Senses of God*, 2nd edn Oxford, One World, 1995, pp. 5f.

7   Tyndall, J., *Fragments of Science*. London, 1889, II, p. 197.

8   Melville, H., letter to N. Hawthorne. In Hayford, H., and Parker, H. (eds.), *Moby Dick*. New York, Norton, 1967, p. 559.

9   Kingsley, F. (ed.), *Charles Kingsley: His Letters and Memories of his Life, edited by his wife*. London, 1877, I, pp. 280f.

10 Kingsley, C., *Yeast: A Problem*. In *Collected Works*. London, 1851, II, p. 82.

11 Aiken, J., *A Description of the Country from Thirty to Forty Miles Round Manchester*, 1795.

12 Arnold wrote those words originally in 1880, in the Introduction to T. H. Ward's *The English Poets*, reprinted as 'The Study of Poetry', in *Essays in Criticism*, Second Series, 1888.

13 Arnold, M., *Literature and Dogma*, Preface to the edn of 1873, p. 4, the last words of which in the edn of 1883 are, 'Miracles do not happen.'

14 Strauss, D. F. In Zeller, E. (ed.), *Ausgewahlte Briefe*, 1895, p. 103.

15 Newman, J. H., The mission of St Bernard. *Historical Sketches*, 11, 1872-3.

16 'Grief! O eternal grief! My father, O, just once more resume the sacred task: live, live, and let me perish.'

17 'I do not know what sin he committed there: he sought atonement for it, yes, holy would he be.'

18 'Acknowledge your fault and then it is ended, by knowledge your folly is mended.'

19 Ascham, M., A very human epic. In John, N. (ed.), *Parsifal*. London, Calder, 1986, pp. 8-10.

20 Tanner, M., The total work of art. In Burbidge, P., and Sutton R. (eds.), *The Wagner Companion*. London, Faber, 1979, p. 209.

21 Quoted from Millington, B., *Wagner*, London, Dent, 1986, pp. 267f.

22 Whitman, W., When I heard the learn'd astronomer. In Holloway, E. (ed.), *Complete Poetry*. London, Nonesuch, 1964, p. 250.

23 Stephen, Sir Leslie, Religion as a fine art. In *Essays on Freethinking and Plainspeaking*, 1873.

24 See Poupard, P. (ed.), *Galileo Galilei: Toward a Resolution of 350 Years of Debate*, 1633-1983, Pittsburgh, Duquesne University Press, 1987.

25 For an explanation of somatic exploration and its relation to religions, see my *Is God a Virus? Genes, Culture and Religion*, London, SPCK, 1995, pp. 151ff.

26 Traherne, T., The third century, 41. In Margoliouth, H. M., (ed.), *Centuries, Poems and Thanksgivings*, 1. Oxford, Clarendon Press, 1972, p. 134.

Chapter Eight: Is Science the New Religion?

1 Hawking, S., *A Brief History of Time*. London, Bantam, 1988.
2 Davies, P., *The Mind of God*. London, Simon & Schuster, 1992.
3 Barrow, J., *Theories of Everything*. Oxford, Clarendon Press, 1991.
4 Tipler, F. J., *The Physics of Immortality*. Basingstoke, Macmillan, 1994,
5 Barrow, *Theories of Everything*, p.11.

Chapter Nine: The God Who Is With the World

1 Vasoli, Cesare, The Renaissance concept of philosophy. In Schmitt, C. B. and Skinner, Q. (eds.), *The Cambridge History of Renaissance Philosophy*. Cambridge, Cambridge University Press, 1988, p. 61.
2 Ecclesiasticus (Ben Sirach) 24.28.
3 O'Siadhail, Micheal, 'Glimpse', in *A Fragile City*. Newcastle, Bloodaxe Books, 1995, p. 77.
4 *Summa Theologiae: A Concise Translation*, ed. Timothy McDermott. Westminster, MD, Christian Classics, 1989, Vol. 1, 3, p.2.
5 *Summa Theologiae: A Concise Translation*. Vol. 5, 199, 9, p. 53.
6 Rupp, E. G. and Drewery, Benjamin (eds.), *Martin Luther*. London, Edward Arnold, 1970, p. 6.
7 Augustine, *The Trinity*, trans. Edmund Hill. Brooklyn, NY, New City Press, 1991. Book II, 14, 16.
8 In practice, they are important to each other. Another discipline may be used to identify and to analyse the subject-matter of the primary discipline. For example, in theology, literary disciplines are used to identify normative sources of Christian faith as 'texts' or 'narrative' or 'rhetoric', and techniques drawn from such disciplines are then used to analyse the sources so construed. Likewise, historical disciplines identify these normative sources as history, social ones identify them as social products, philosophical disciplines 'ideas' or 'problems', and so forth, and in each case the relevant disciplines are then applied.

Such practices are often despised by those who claim the possibility of a more purified access to their subject-matter. In theology, the truth of sources and normative interpretations is considered distinct and self-interpreting, and therefore beyond understanding in categories drawn from interdisciplinary studies. The Bible is not 'texts', but the Word of God; God is God; sin is to be understood only by reference to the holiness of God and redemption in Christ; philosophy is to serve the truth of theology; and so on. If analogies are drawn with other subject-matter or disciplines, dualistic, paradoxical and dialogical or contrastive forms of thought are used to characterize the utter difference of the normative truths of Christian faith. Whether tacitly or explicitly, it is claimed that theological research should be occupied with the purity of the tradition understood ever more deeply in its own terms.

9 Walsh, D., *After Ideology*. San Francisco, HarperSanFrancisco, 1990, p. 183.

10 Nerburn, K. and Mengelkoch, L. (eds.), *Native American Wisdom*. Novato, CA, New World Library, 1991, p. 1.

11 Weinberg, S., *Dreams of a Final Theory*. New York, Pantheon Books, 1992, pp. 244–5.

12 Torrance, A. J., *Persons in Communion: Trinitarian Description and Human Participation*. Edinburgh, T&T Clark, 1996, p. 314. The book makes these remarks in the context of a discussion of the dynamics of revelation, not in the wide one to which we apply them here.

13 O'Siadhail, Micheal, 'Perspectives', in *The Chosen Garden*. Dublin, The Daedelus Press, 1991, p. 86. Reprinted in *Hail! Modern Jazz*. Newcastle, Bloodaxe Books, 1992, p. 126.

14 Thus from the implicit rationality of 'the Father', the Spirit can be seen to generate the fullness of the Father through the Son and through the Son's work in the world.

FURTHER READING

General

Barbour, I. G.	*Religion in an Age of Science.* London, SCM Press, 1990.
Drees, W. B.	*Religion, Science and Naturalism.* Cambridge University Press, 1996.
Fuller, M.*	*Atoms and Icons.* London, Mowbray, 1995.
Haught, J. F.*	*Science and Religion: From Conflict to Conversation.* New York, Paulist Press, 1995.
Holder, R. D.*	*Nothing but Atoms and Molecules: Probing the Limits of Science.* Tunbridge Wells, Monarch, 1993.
Peacocke, A. R.*	*God and Science: A Quest for Christian Credibility.* London, SCM Press, 1996.
Peacocke, A. R.	*Theology for a Scientific Age.* London, SCM Press, 1993.
Polkinghorne, J.*	*Quarks, Chaos and Christianity.* London, SPCK, 1994.
Richardson, W. M. & Wildman, W. J. (eds.)	*Religion and Science: History, Method, Dialogue.* London, Routledge, 1996.

Physics and Cosmology

Davies, P.*	*The Mind of God: Science and the Search for Ultimate Meaning.* Harmondsworth, Penguin, 1993.
Drees, W.*	*Beyond the Big Bang.* La Salle, Open Court, 1990.
Stannard, R.*	*Doing Away with God? Creation and the Big Bang.* London, Marshall Pickering, 1993.
Tilby, A.*	*Science and the Soul: New Cosmology, the Self and God.* London, SPCK, 1992.
Wilkinson, D.*	*God, the Big Bang and Stephen Hawking.* Tunbridge Wells, Monarch, 1993.

| Worthing, M. W. | *God, Creation and Contemporary Physics.* Minneapolis, Fortress Press, 1996. |

Biological and Human Sciences

Hefner, P.	*The Human Factor: Evolution, Culture and Religion.* Minneapolis, Fortress Press, 1993.
Jeeves, M.	*Human Nature at the Millennium.* Grand Rapids, Baker Books/Leicester, Apollos, 1997.
Midgeley, M.*	*Evolution as Religion.* London, Methuen, 1985.
Peacocke, A.	*God and the New Biology.* London, Dent, 1986. (reprinted Gloucester, MA., Peter Smith)
Puddefoot, J.*	*God and the Mind Machine.* London, SPCK, 1996.

History

| Brooke, J. H. | *Science and Religion: Some Historical Perspectives.* Cambridge, Cambridge University Press, 1991. |
| Russell, C. | *Cross-Currents: Interactions Between Science and Faith.* Leicester, Inter-varsity Press, 1985. |

Philosophy

van Huyssteen, W.	*Theology and the Justification of Faith.* Grand Rapids, Eerdmans, 1989.
Midgeley, M.*	*Science as Salvation.* London, Routledge, 1992.
Murphy, N.	*Theology in the Age of Scientific Reasoning.* Ithica, Cornell University Press, 1990.
Ward, K.*	*God, Chance and Necessity.* Oxford, One World, 1996.

Theology

Gilkey, L.	*Nature, Reality and the Sacred: The Nexus of Science and Religion.* Minneapolis, Fortress Press, 1993.
Pannenberg, W.	*Towards a Theology of Nature: Essays on Science and Faith.* Louisville, Westminster John Knox Press, 1993.
Polkinghorne, J. C.	*Science and Christian Belief.* London, SPCK, 1994.

* Suitable for introductory reading

INDEX